For Russell

Ted Spratt

FINANCIAL PLANNING
For Good Times and Bad Times

FINANCIAL PLANNING
For Good Times and Bad Times

Ted Spratt

The Book Guild Ltd.
Sussex, England

This book is sold subject to the condition that is shall not, by way of trade or otherwise, be lent, re-sold, hired out, photocopied or held in any retrieval system or otherwise circulated without the publisher's prior consent in any form of binding or cover other than that in which this is published and without a similar condition including this condition being imposed on the subsequent purchaser.

The Book Guild Ltd.
25 High Street,
Lewes, Sussex.

First published 1992
© Ted Spratt 1992
Set in Baskerville
Typesetting by Southern Reproductions (Sussex)
East Grinstead, Sussex.
Printed in Great Britain by
Antony Rowe Ltd.
Chippenham, Wiltshire.

A catalogue record for this book is
available from the British Library

ISBN 0 86332 675 7

A Financial Adviser's job is to help his or her clients to discover and define their goals and to help them understand the problems they face in reaching their stated goals.

This book is intended as a source of information and is designed to help readers to ask the right questions and understand the answers together with general indications of advantageous financial strategies.

It is not intended to be a source of specific advice and you are asked not to act upon any of the information or ideas contained in the following pages without previous discussion with a Financial Adviser. In many cases it has been found that apparently simple cases are not so when properly analysed.

Often in fact, the most simple of situations contain many hidden traps for the unwary. This means that full information must be disclosed to your Financial Adviser before any action can be recommended. To ensure added protection for clients we have developed a fail safe computer system to ensure that all areas are fully covered before advice is given.

We disclaim any liability for action taken or not taken on the information contained in this book.

To Roy

CONTENTS

Preface		9
1. Ted Spratt: Who's He?		11
2. Why Should I Read This Book?		19
3. Why Do I Need A Financial Plan?		37
4. What Will Happen To My Family When I Die?		47
5. What Will Happen To Me And My Family If I Suffer Long Term Illness?		58
6. What Will Happen To Me If I Live To Retirement?		62
7. How Do I Make The Most Of My Investments?		70
8. Who Will Inherit My Assets When I Die?		84
9. Will The Taxman Be My Main Beneficiary When I Die? – Simple Will Planning		90
10. Simple Use Of Flexible Trusts		100
11. How Do I Arrange My Affairs Both For Life And Death? – My Personal Business Plan		107
12. What Should I Expect From My Financial Adviser?		112
13. What Do I Do When Someone Dies?		126
Helpful Booklets		135
Appendix i	Widows and Widowers	138
Appendix ii	Mortgages	141
Appendix iii	Taxed Growth Versus Non Taxed Growth	147
Appendix iv	Income Protection	149
Appendix v	Investment Delay	151
Appendix vi	Aims of the Book	153
Appendix vii	General Comments	155
Appendix viii	The Story Behind The Figures	157

PREFACE

Dream-Maker

The more we are surrounded by high-tech equipment, the more we need the personal touch. Never having grown up, I love electronic gimmickry: new computers, new programmes, electronic organizers, calculator/alarm clocks, etc. However, I only use them to educate myself, not to impress my clients.

It is important to have and to use the latest equipment, but, like a garden fork, they are only tools: tools to do the job required of them. They are therefore used to save time, to number crunch, to try out the various 'instances' that will enable me to tailor-make proposals that the client will feel are personal to him and fit his needs. After all, our job is to turn 'dreams' into reality.

I have never sold insurance – nobody wants insurance. I just talk to people about their circumstances: about what they want out of life and what their dreams are. Even more importantly, I listen to what they say, because I want to help them achieve their ideal, their fantasy.

For example, I recently went to see a prospective client who had no capital, and whose income almost matched his outgoings. Yet he had a dream, a dream to own a Greek taverna on one of the Greek islands when he retired in twenty-three years time. He thought it was only a dream, no more than a vague wish or hope, for he never believed that it was possible.

Together we are restructuring his finances, and setting out a programme which should enable him to achieve his dreams.

The effect is already startling: he feels more alive, and for the first time in his life, he is not only taking an active interest in his finances, but he is actually enjoying them. This is because he now understands his money; the mysticism has gone; he is now out of the maze.

Now he realizes that good effective financial planning, actively monitored, can give him what he once thought was an unattainable dream. He knows that if he tries hard enough, his 'fantasy' will come true. Even if, for some reason, he does not achieve his dream, he will have enjoyed the journey. He will have had a better and more fulfilling life, and can look forward to a more financially secure retirement.

He will not have failed. He will not have failed because

'SUCCESS IS NOT JUST A DESTINATION,
IT IS ALSO A JOURNEY'

1

TED SPRATT - WHO'S HE?
or
HOW I FELL FOR
THE LIFE ASSURANCE INDUSTRY

I am a professional financial adviser who decided to write this book about my experiences before and after I joined the Financial Services Industry. To me there was a need for a book which could explain, in simple terms, the importance of planning personal finance and how to make the most of one's assets.

The aims of the book are to dispel the myths and mystery of Finance, to demonstrate the fundamental need for everyone to have a sound Financial Plan, together with the necessity of obtaining good professional financial advice. Even more importantly it shows the penalties of not planning your finances.

WHY I BECAME A FINANCIAL ADVISER

Up to the age of thirty-one I was very fit and healthy and had a highly profitable retail children's wear business, selling through market stalls and shops.

I did not believe in insurance. Why should I? There was nothing wrong with me so I had no need for any protection, at least so I thought.

THE DAY THE WORLD COLLAPSED

Then I fell through the ceiling at home (all I was doing was insulating the loft, just an ordinary everyday simple job).

The timing was perfect as my wife was pregnant with our third child within three years (imagine coping with three babies in napkins and a cripple for a husband together with a business that would not run itself).

The result of this one 'small' slip was fourteen years of pain for me and misery for the whole family. It finally led to the closing of a very good business, together with some very expensive medical bills and eventually the loss of every penny saved. Just six more months and we would have been homeless.

If I had thought to plan I could have protected my income so that although my business would still have failed my own and my family's standard of living would not have reduced or at least only a little. My savings would also still have been more or less intact.

No one told me (or if they did, I did not listen) that I could have arranged for the best in the medical world to operate quickly and at my convenience.

I did not realize that not only could I have taken out a private pension but I could also have had the contributions protected so that when I was unable to work my pension would have continued, just as if I was still at work and able to make the payments; thus ensuring a reasonable standard of living in my retirement.

I did not know that I could have started a life policy – and again had the contributions protected in the case of illness or injury. Nor did I realize that I could have arranged for my mortgage payments to be paid for me whilst I was incapacitated.

I DID NOT   I WOULD NOT LISTEN
DO YOU KNOW?   DO YOU REALIZE?
HAVE YOU LISTENED?

I agree the above protection would not have solved all our problems but at least my wife and three children would not have suffered financially as well as emotionally.

When I was eventually back to normal (well almost), I joined the Life Assurance Industry. After a while I began to see things as I had never seen them before. This new viewpoint has enabled me to help prevent the same financial problems that have occurred in my life from happening to my clients.

So, many years down the line, this book has been written.

My accident could have killed me. What would have happened to my family then? True there would have been no medical fees but: what would the business have been worth, without the driving force? My wife would have become my widow (the word widow comes from the ancient language Sanskrit, it means EMPTY), how would she have managed with two babies and one on the way?

Remember I had no protection against anything. All I had was my conceit that nothing major would ever happen, to ME. I was different (or so I thought).

For example: I would never have a car accident, after all I was a careful driver. I only protected my car because it was legally required. I never protected the driver's life because it was not law.

Yet which was the most important – the car or the driver?. Which would be the easiest and cheapest to replace – the car or the driver?

I never thought of myself or my family.

I never planned for the future in any way. When I wanted and needed to protect my income, it was too late; I could not, I was uninsurable. I was too great a risk for the insurance companies to insure.

Yet if I had insured myself before I needed any protection then it would have cost very little. It would have been the best financial investment I could have made.

The trouble with protection policies is you have to take them out before you need them. Once you need them it is too late, they are unobtainable.

This means that you have to plan for what may happen – rather than assume that nothing will happen. It may cost money to take out insurance but it can cost far more if you don't, both in financial and emotional terms.

As Winston Churchill said:

'If I had my way I would write the word "INSURE" upon the door of every cottage and upon the blotting book of every public man. Because I am convinced that for the sacrifices which are inconceivably small families and estates can be protected against catastrophes which would otherwise smash them up for ever. It is our duty to arrest the ghastly waste, not merely of human happiness but of national health and strength which follows when, through the death of the breadwinner, the frail boat in which the family are embarked flounders and women and children and estates are left to struggle in the dark waters of a friendless world.'

I found out the hard way what Winston Churchill meant. Will you find out the hard way?

I did have the chance to protect myself and my family but I did not take it.

Do you still have a chance to protect yourself and your family? If so, are you going to risk losing your chance?

It is one of life's more unpleasant facts that you never know the true value of anything, until you lose it.

WHAT COULD I HAVE DONE TO PROTECT MYSELF AND MY FAMILY?

I could have seen a professional financial adviser who would have explained the potential problems and how to plan for them.

For example: for a small monthly outlay I could have purchased an Income Protection Policy to give me up to three-quarters of my income, indexed in line with average earnings until age 65.

I could have arranged for a Life Protection Policy to give my wife and family sufficient tax-free capital which if invested wisely would have provided my widow with the same standard of living for the rest of her life. It would also have allowed her to bring up the children in the way I would have liked (I cannot say planned because we had no real, actual plans, just a vague 'yes we would like that'). It could also have helped to give the children a start in life.

This type of plan (whole of life) builds up a cash value. If I had not died, by age sixty-five I could have continued with the policy or taken a tax-free lump sum.

Again, for a similar amount, I could have arranged for private medical treatment for the whole family. I know the NHS is supposed to give what is needed but if you want the best attention *when* you need it you have to be prepared to pay. I do not like the fact, I do not agree with the fact, but unfortunately it is a fact.

I did not, yet I could have paid for this protection without even noticing the outgoings.

The same would have applied to my pension; *if* I had had one.

But I did not have a professional financial adviser nor did I understand what a financial adviser was, nor did I realize what a good financial adviser could do for his or her clients.

WHAT IS A GOOD FINANCIAL ADVISER?

Here I think it is better to say first what a good financial adviser is NOT.

> They are not usually a: Accountant, Solicitor, Stockbroker, Building Society Manager, Bank Manager or Estate Agent. Nor are they a new member of the Life Assurance Industry.

Each of the above has his or her own specialist skills that are connected closely with finance but all are engaged in full time occupations; it is impossible for them to have the necessary skills to do both jobs properly. Having said that, each has a part to play in any Financial Plan.

Some larger firms of solicitors and accountants have realized this an as a result have started to develop specialist divisions. Unfortunately this seldom works correctly as they consist of a rigid structure with centralized expertise (to reduce costs), or they have a centralized recommended list. In other words everyone receives the same advice which cuts out the essential personal touch.

A Financial Adviser is a recent development from the old type of Life Assurance/Investment Adviser. He or she is someone who has been in the Financial Services Industry for several years, has seen life and understands the problems that can and do occur, no matter how carefully we plan, throughout life. Above all they are someone who takes time; time to listen, to understand your individual problems and concerns. They will talk, ask questions to help guide you in the direction you wish to go.

Above all Financial Advisers must understand their own limitations and be able to call on the expertise of other professionals to integrate their skills into your overall plan. In other words, the Financial Adviser must be a central co-ordinator.

There is an old saying, *'The more you know the more you realize you don't know'*: how true it is.

So a Financial Adviser is someone who assists you to plan your finances for now and the future and who helps you rectify any past errors and build on past successes or even failures.

It is an adviser's job to advise and guide you around life's potential problems, to help lead you and/or your family to a financially sound future.

Financial Advisers (by law) come in two guises:
       1. Tied Agents   2. Independent Advisers

1. TIED AGENTS OR APPOINTED REPRESENTATIVES

A Tied Agent works for an insurance company. He or she can only work for just one Life Assurance company (or a company that only recommends and sells the products of only one Life Assurance company). They are not allowed, BY LAW, to discuss or recommend any other Life Assurance company's products. Their recommendations are monitored by the Life Assurance company concerned. They are trained to a high technical standard and tested by that insurance company. The insurance company is closely monitored by the Life Assurance Unit Trust Regulatory Organization (LAUTRO).

The Financial Services Act (FSA) 1986, requires tied agents to put forward the most suitable product in that company's range.

2. INDEPENDENT FINANCIAL ADVISERS

An Independent Financial Adviser works for YOU. NOT an Insurance company.

An Independent Financial Adviser is required BY LAW not only to recommend the ideal product for your needs but ALSO the best Insurance Company for that product.

Their recommendations are monitored by a totally independent body – usually the Financial Intermediaries, Managers and Brokers Regulatory Association (FIMBRA).

Strangely there is not a competence test nor any form of examination for an Independent Adviser. He or she is judged to be fully competent once he or she has been in the industry for two years. Before that time has elapsed their recommendations have to be checked by an authorized member of FIMBRA.

Both types of advisers have to give you, again BY LAW, a copy of the 'BUYER'S GUIDE' at the first meeting. This 'BUYER'S GUIDE' will explain your adviser's status. A recent survey (February 1991) has shown that only around 15 per cent of tied advisers and 25 per cent of independents do give out these guides.

Most banks and building societies are not independent; they are tied to one insurance company, and therefore are only able to recommend the products of that particular insurance company. For example, if you are not happy with the lack of choice from your potential lender on requesting an endowment or pension mortgage you can insist on seeing a Professional Financial Adviser to arrange the endowment or pension. Your Adviser will also be able to select the best lending source whether it be a bank or a building society for your mortgage or other type of loan.

Many people do not realize that there is no legal requirement to buy your insurance product from the mortgage lender. Most banks and building societies have, or are in the process of, setting up their own independent arm to cater for the more financially aware. But it is seldom, as yet, that they can cater for this freedom of choice on the spot.

CHOOSE YOUR FINANCIAL ADVISER VERY CAREFULLY
DO NOT BUY OFF THE PAGE OR BECAUSE OF
A SPECIAL OFFER
YOUR FUTURE IS TOO IMPORTANT

2

WHY SHOULD I READ THIS BOOK?

'There are no conditions to which man cannot become accustomed, especially if he sees all around him living in the same way'
                                        Leo Tolstoy

This book has been written to help you to create a suitable environment to allow you to plan your financial future through the good times – and even more importantly through the bad times – and to help you change your unfulfilled financial expectations into reality.

It will talk about death, disability (these two first as they can happen at any time) and living, the problems that can and do occur throughout life, and it will help you to prepare a strategy to protect you and your family from, and guide you round, many of these problems. Remember there are two things guaranteed in life 'DEATH AND TAXES'.

The book is designed to help you fully realize the importance of Financial Planning, of using a good Financial Adviser, what he or she is and how to choose one.

It will explain why you MUST write a Will (and keep it up to date). More importantly it will show you the penalties of not writing a Will.

Trusts will be explained and you will be shown how and when to use them.

Many misconceptions about the Life Assurance Industry will be removed. Help will be given in how to assess whether or not you need any life protection, if so why you need it and how much you need.

But, the basic reason it has been written is because of my

own experiences both before and after I joined the industry.

As I said earlier, when I first joined the Financial Services industry I found that few people, like myself, had any form of organized financial plan for their future or knew just where they are or want to be, financially. After a few years I have prepared my own statistics from my first reviews of potential clients' insurance type policies.

The figures are astounding and frightening:

* 91 per cent needed some form of modification or amendment.

* 87 per cent needed to have the client's age proved.

* 75 per cent of Life Protection Policies should have been placed into Trust at outset – 87 per cent of these were placed into Trust on my first review.

* 90 per cent of Personal Pension Funds should have been placed into Trust at outset – 99 per cent of them were placed into Trust on my first review.

* 13 per cent of Savings type life policies should have been placed into Trust at outset – few, because of changes in legislation, were placed into Trust on my first review.

* 68 per cent of Executive type pensions were not set up correctly – because of the lack of communication between the Company's solicitor and it's pensions adviser, this will be explained fully in the business version of the book which is to follow shortly.

* 81 per cent of Partnerships have no protection for the partners.

* 69 per cent of Private Limited Companies have no Director of Share protection.

* 78 per cent of Firms have no protection for their Key People.

* 76 per cent of clients had no Will – 19 per cent of those with a Will needed it to be modified in some way or rewritten, my figures are higher than are normally quoted (all the other figures I have seen, say around 60 per cent do not have Wills). The reason for my higher figure is threefold:

   1. I do not count Do It Yourself Wills as true Wills.

   2. Nor do I count the Will forms that are bought for 50p.

   3. A surprising number of people have had a Will written correctly yet have never actually signed it.

* No mortgages were planned in an Inheritance Tax efficient manner.

At our first meeting many people made comments like: 'I do not like to talk about it,' or, 'I don't intend dying, yet. My wife' (he means his widow) 'will be all right if I die, the State will look after her; the family will look after the children; she can get a job; she can remarry.' All these may be true – but is it really what you want to happen?

Some of these statements may be true, but they are only ways of avoiding the unpleasant. People do die; mortality is 100 per cent per person; it is not a matter of *if* you will die but *when* you will die, so you do need to plan for it. You may have thirty years to plan for your retirement, but not even thirty minutes to plan for your death.

Families are left with many problems that only money can solve. Widows do have financial as well as emotional problems. Money does reduce financial problems and therefore also helps with the emotional trauma. The presence of money means one problem less.

---

* For the full story and meaning of the above figures turn to Appendix viii.

It is therefore the breadwinner's job to see that his or her family is looked after financially whether he or she is here or not.

If you went abroad for twelve months, would you leave your family with little or no financial support?

However, many people die and death lasts forever, not just for twelve months) and leave their family with little or no support.

As one widow said:

> *'Like it or not the first thing I had to set right was money.'*

> *'At times, although I loved Martin, I found myself starting to hate him for not thinking of us.'*

> *'He loved us, he would not have wanted this to happen.'*

But it did happen.
She also said:

> *'It was not his fault. he just didn't think, he just did not realize.'*

Was she right?   If so, WHOSE FAULT WAS IT?
HIS ADVISER'S?   HER'S?

Again, your future and your family's future is your responsibility whether you are here or not.

And it is your Financial Adviser's job to help you fulfil that responsibility.

At times, from this point, the book may seem to be sexist to some readers. It is sexist because the world, unfortunately, is still sexist (I hope that this will have changed by the time the next version of this book is due).

At the moment it is a fact that women suffer both emotionally and financially more than men do on the death of their spouse. Men are still the dominant sex but this is changing rapidly. Although I hope men and women reach the stage of equality I dread the thought of the sexes being the 'same' as some agitators seem to wish.

THE SIZE OF THE PROBLEM

IN THE EVENT OF THE DEATH OF THE BREADWINNER

Look what is happening to people and their families in the UK:

TODAY

over 700 people will die

over 450 wives will become widows

over 200 husbands will become widowers

Out of every 100 men aged 25 alive today, by age 65

25 will be dead

3 out of 4 widows remarry for financial reasons

6 out of 10 families have financial problems immediately the breadwinner dies

9 out of 10 families have serious financial problems within a year of the death of the breadwinner

The average breadwinner has enough life protection to look after their family for less than two years

IN RETIREMENT

Statement: 'I have a pension.'
Reply: 'Yes, but how much is it?'

Much less than you think in nine cases out of ten. If you wait until you retire to find out, it will be too late.

Statement: 'The State will look after me.'
Reply: 'Yes, I am sure they will.'

BUT LOOK AT THE FACTS! LOOK WHAT IS HAPPENING TODAY!

See how people living today have looked after themselves and their families:

Out of every 100 men aged 25 alive today, by age 65:

One will be wealthy

Four will be well-to-do

Sixteen will be self supporting or working

Fifty-four will be dependent on the State or relations

Twenty-five will be dead

These figures are frightening but now look at the figures for ladies:

Out of every 100 ladies aged 25 alive today, by age 60:

None will be wealthy

One will be well-to-do

Ten will be self supporting or working

Seventy-eight will be dependent on the State or relations

Eleven will be dead

85 out of every 100 people aged 75 or over do not have £150 of spendable income per week.

90 out of every 100 deaths after age 65 can be partially traced to financial worries.

One third of all senior citizens live below the poverty line.

Where the head of household is over the age of 65:

66 per cent have an income of less than £99 per week

Yet during their working life a fortune will have passed through their hands. A person aged 25 now earning £6000 will have by age 65 earned the staggering sum of £999,999, assuming just a 7.5 per cent increase in salary.
How much will he have left to show for it?

£1 a day invested now (into a personal pension, assumed growth 12 per cent) will mean £148 per day, for life, when the investor retires at age 65.

This means that it is not so much a question of: *How much have I earned?* but far more a question of: *How much have I saved?* And of: *How much is it worth?*

Study the effect of inflation on the purchasing power of money in your pocket:

£1000 in 1967 was worth just £644 by 1977, and by 1987 just £180. What will it be worth in 1997?

PROLONGED ILLNESS

Statement: 'I do not intend being ill.'
Statement: 'I am fit and healthy.'
Statement: 'It will not happen to me.'
These statements are made by people today but look how these people are looking after themselves and their families. (Remember how I looked after myself and my family?)

EVERYDAY IN THE UK:
Over 2700 people will start to claim sickness benefit
Over 850,000 people have been sick or disabled for over one year
Over 100,000 people have been sick or disabled and unable to work
for over ten years

Both as a person and as a Financial Adviser, I became very worried about the above facts.

Both as a person and as a Financial Adviser, I became very concerned that most members of the public I met could fall into the above traps (remember what happened to me and my family)?

They did not know where they were financially, nor where they wished to be (except in some vague form 'I would like to be well off some day'). Hence the popularity of the Pools: 'Why plan when I can get a fortune by investing a penny – after all one person in fifty million wins a fortune.' By all means have a flutter on the Pools but **DO NOT RELY** on them for your financial future. You need to provide the bread and butter yourself: let the Pools give you the jam, if you are lucky.

It is frightening that most of the readers of this book just do not realize, and even more frightening that their Financial Advisers do not tell them.

Your Financial Adviser should tell you about the problems your widow and children might suffer, but need not suffer if you plan ahead.

Strange that we have a word for children if they lose both parents but not if they only lose one parent.

You probably do not realize, you are not told of the

problems that can and do occur. You forget what insurance policies you have, and all too often I could only find out by reference to that person's bank statements, and then by writing to the insurance companies for details. On one occasion on writing to an insurance company about a client's policy they informed me that an endowment had matured two years previously with a value of over £57,000; the company had written to the client but he had changed address so never received the letter. Until I told him he was not aware of this money (sorry but I cannot guarantee to do that for all my clients).

Often, as the above illustration shows, clients do not remember why they started policies, when they matured, which company they were with, nor where the documents were kept.

They do not know what they were worth, now or on maturity, in cash terms, or even more importantly adjusted for inflation, whether or not they were in trust, or the reason for being or not being in trust.

Many of you will not know whether your policies are age admitted, why they should be age admitted, or even what it means, nor whether the policies are still sufficient – and what of inflation?

Seldom are you told clearly how, or even if, your policies fit into any overall financial picture.

IS IT YOUR FAULT?
OR
IS IT THE FAULT OF YOUR 'FINANCIAL ADVISER'

for not warning you of these problems, and then not guiding you round the potential pitfalls?

Why should you plan?

Simply to ensure that your wishes for your own and your family's financial future are achieved: whether you live, die, or become totally disabled.

Life is very much like a tightrope – one slip can lead to financial disaster. But safety nets can be arranged: at whatever

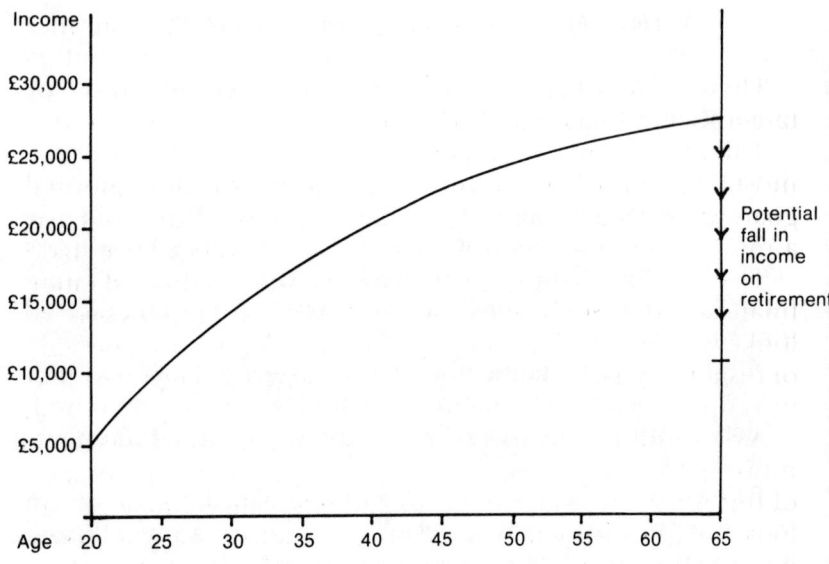

height and to whatever standard you require, wherever and whenever you need them, or to fit within your budget. If you reach the end of the tightrope (retirement) you should have the safety net of an adequate pension linked to inflation.

To bring home the importance of sound financial planning for the future I have, over the years, developed a recording and planning system that ensures that my clients have their own:

PERSONAL FINANCIAL BUSINESS PLAN

This Business Plan enables my clients to know:

WHERE THEY ARE

WHERE THEY ARE GOING

HOW TO GET THERE

THE COST OF GETTING THERE

and even more importantly:

THE COST OF NOT GETTING THERE

They know: whether or not they are on target, ahead of target, behind target and what to do in each event.

True, they may not all achieve all of their ambitions, but most of them will. Even those who do not achieve all their goals will still have enjoyed the planning and will at least have a more financially secure future than they would have had.

They are told: how their families will be looked after financially when they die; how they and their families will be looked after financially if they become sick for a long period, or disabled. Clients know: what their standard of living will be in retirement.

As a result of this involvement, my clients start to take a more active part in their own financial planning, and because of this, they start to understand and enjoy their finances and look forward to their regular reviews with at least as much input from them as from me.

They learn about their problems, and more importantly, how to prevent or how to solve them.

Not all are willing or able to do enough about it, but at least they will be able to make a start.

They will never be able to say:

> 'You did not tell me that I would not have enough to live on comfortably in retirement.'

Their family will not be able to say:

> 'We did not know that we would not have enough money to live on when the breadwinner died.'

or that

> 'We did not know that we would have to sell our home to have enough money to live on.'

This book does not seek to take the place of your Financial Adviser: indeed it cannot. What it will do is help you realize the importance of Financial Planning and the importance of good professional financial advice.

It will help you find out where you are and where you want to be financially – but you will still need your Financial Adviser to tell you how to get there.

It will guide you in what to look for in your Financial Adviser and help you decide how good your current Financial Adviser is. But it will not replace a good Financial Adviser.

In fact nowhere in this book will you find any recommendations other than:

To ACT and ACT NOW

and consult a Professional Adviser

You must plan. The most important thing is to start to plan . . . and to start to plan *NOW*.

Remember it has been said many times, by many people, that:

'PEOPLE DO NOT PLAN TO FAIL, THEY JUST FAIL TO PLAN.'

You will find that once you start to plan, you start to be successful. The journey to your financial destination will become interesting, exciting and incredibly rewarding, both in a financial and emotional way.

You and your family will reap the reward of paving the way to your own and your family's financial security and happiness in the future. You will start to enjoy your money.

Finance frightens people but it is really only a fear of the unknown. This fear will disappear as knowledge increases; it's a bit like being in a darkened room and being told there is a deep hole in the floor. You are scared to move, until you switch on the light, and then all your fears disappear just because you can see, and therefore analyse, your problem and find a way round it.

Once you have organized, and fully understand, your finances, it becomes a little like looking down on a maze: you can see just where the difficulties are likely to be and therefore how to go round them and see the way to reach your destination.

This knowledge will give you and your family a great feeling of well-being and peace of mind.

Three of my favourite statements are:

> *'One-off financial planning is about as useless as one-off family planning. Little mistakes occur that grow bigger and more expensive every day.'*

> *'If you do not know where you are financially, how can you get to where you want to be financially?'*

and

> *'Financial planning is a process, not a product.'*

As I said earlier, when I first joined the Financial Services Industry I found that many people were just sold a policy with little or no regard for their individual needs; the policy was just something which only fitted in with the rest of their finances. If it did, then it was by accident and not design.

Again, I must repeat how surprised I was at how few people had any form of financial plan for their future, even those people who were otherwise financially aware. Too few financial advisers explained, in simple language, what was needed, and why. I must say here that not everybody is willing to listen, nor do some clients make it easy for the financial adviser to explain details.

The majority of people have a series of unrelated investments, savings or life policies, but with (as I have said before) little or no idea of just what policies they have, why they have them, or any tax implications.

Most people have little knowledge of their current financial position, nor any real idea as to where they would like to be in the future, and therefore, obviously, no formal plan to achieve future financial security. On asking them what they thought would happen in the future, common answers were, *'Well, the company will give us a pension,'* or *'the State will look after us.'*

True financial planning is a very much neglected subject, because most people assume (like Inheritance Tax) that it is only for the very rich. The latter often don't plan *because* they are very wealthy, and therefore feel that they have no need to plan ahead.

Neither of these statements are true. It is equally important for everyone, no matter what their current financial status. In fact, if anything, it could be argued that the less money you have, the more you need to plan for your future, since each £ saved represents a larger proportion of your estate.

Why should you plan?

To ensure your and your family's financial future if:
a) you are disabled, either through illness or accident,
b) if you live to retirement,
c) or to ensure your family's financial future when you die (not, 'if' you die, mortality is 100 per cent per person).
Financial planning is a job for today, not tomorrow. It is never too early to start the plan – the later you start, the steeper the climb, and the greater the cost.

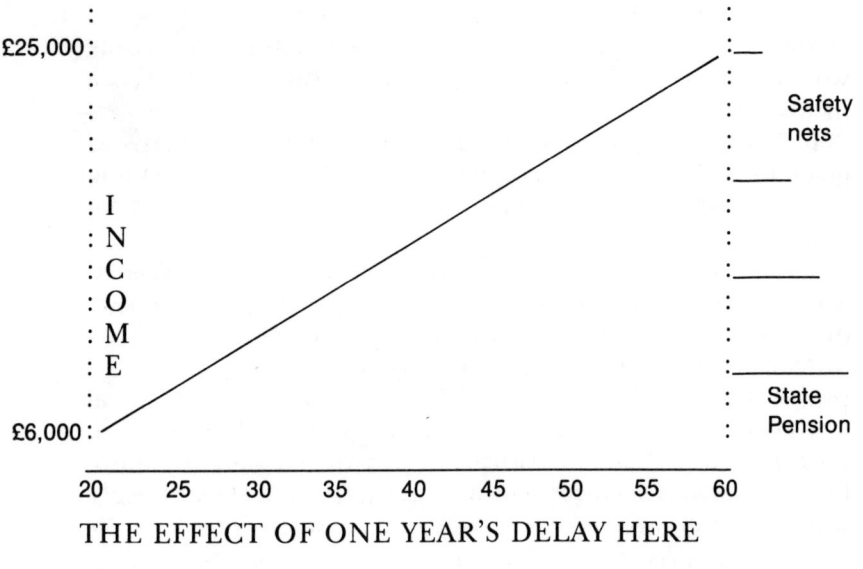

THE EFFECT OF ONE YEAR'S DELAY HERE

AGE

For example: a man aged thirty-four wanting to invest £500 gross (£375 net) into his pension decides to wait just one more year.

He saves £375, but suffers, by age sixty-five: a reduction in fund value of £27,611 (assuming a modest 12 per cent growth); a reduction in his tax free lump sum of £8494; a reduction in his pension for life of £2523 per year. This means, if he is Mr Average, his total loss of income over the years of his retirement is £43,816 (less, of course, the £375 he did not invest).

As I have already said:
Financial Planning is not a product. Financial Planning is a process.

How do you plan?

Firstly, you need to discover:
1. Where you are financially
2. Where you want to be financially.
   Work out how to get there, and DO IT.
   Simple isn't it?

Your plan of action must be realistic, credible, attainable, workable, and above all flexible. It also needs to be put down in writing, and looked at often.

It needs to be constantly monitored and adjusted. Your goals must be continually reassessed.

BUT the key is to plan, and to start to plan NOW.

It must be realized that financial success is not a destination – it is a journey. Once you start to plan financially, you start to achieve financial success. Once you put your plan into operation you *become* successful.

This simple fact seems to escape both professionals and public alike.

Too many policies have been, and still are, sold without true regard for any short and/or long term financial plan. This also leads to many unsuitable products sold, therefore creating unsatisfied clients.

Always suspect an adviser who recommends the cancellation of a life or investment policy: it is seldom good advice.

It is very important that you know:
   a) what you have

b) why you have it
c) how it fits into your overall plan.

Very often, financial planning has been done with a friend who has just joined the industry (and therefore needs the business); the bank manager; the building society manager; the accountant; a department store; a solicitor; or even through the post, which is even worse, and usually only done because of some incentive, such as a free calculator or clock. The mind boggles – seldom is there any continuity.

This is wrong, indeed very wrong, yet, is the client at fault, or is it the financial industry and its image?

Financial planning should be comprehensive. Everybody should have a fully integrated plan, designed by a professional, based on THEIR OWN personal, current, financial situation. It should be designed to achieve what they wish it to achieve, in the time, and with the finances available, and of course, constantly monitored and modified to meet any changes in their situation or future requirements. It must be totally flexible.

When I visit new clients, no matter how sophisticated they are, (I know I have said this before, and no doubt will again) I am almost always surprised by the fact that they almost never have a truly integrated portfolio, nor any real idea of what they have, why they have it, where it is kept, what it does, or how indeed it fits in with their requirements (if indeed it does), nor do they realize the tax implication of what they have.

To rectify this I have developed a simple, commonsense, approach to financial planning (Spratt's Guide to Financial Planning and Reporting*). The approach involves the use of the different skills of the financial adviser, accountant, stockbroker, bank manager, building society manager, and solicitor, thus making it a totally integrated package that ensures complete co-operation between professionals, instead of confrontation, as is all too often the case now.

It is not possible for you to do so on your own.
IT MUST BE STRESSED AGAIN THAT NO FINANCIAL PLANNING SHOULD BE DONE WITHOUT THE HELP OF A PROFESSIONAL FINANCIAL ADVISER.

---

* this system is available to other professional advisers, either under licence, or on an individual fee basis.

My system can be divided into eight phases: eight steps to financial security.

PHASE 1
Review of Your Current Financial Position

It is necessary to define exactly where you are, whether what you own has a place in your portfolio, whether you have a Will, and if so, is it written properly, is it up to date, and does it do what you want or need to do? Are your policies age admitted?* Are the policies suitable: do they fit into your strategy? Having said this, I stress again that it is seldom good advice to cancel a policy.

Is your policy in trust? In many cases I have found policies are not put into trust, because the tax and time implications of not doing so have not been fully explained to, or understood by, the client.

PHASE 2
Set Goals

Decide where you want to be financially, and how you see yourself in the future.

PHASE 3
Write (re Review) Your Will

See a solicitor and write a Will. The financial and time implications of not writing a Will are nothing short of horrendous.

PHASE 4
Consult Your Professional Financial Adviser

With their help devise the best route to achieve these goals and your financial commitment (nothing worth having costs nothing), or if the goals are unrealistic, either in time, cost or both, ensure that you are aware now of any future shortfall.

PHASE 5
Put It Down On Paper

PHASE 6
DO IT!!

PHASE 7
Prepare a Booklet (along the lines of our guide)

The booklet should have all the information about the phases, PLUS all the information your widow, your advisers and your beneficiaries need to know in the event of your death; all the information you and your professional advisers need to know to maintain your financial plan on track whilst you live, and to assist your executors and other advisers on your death.

PHASE 8
Constantly Reassess

Make sure that you are on target, and if you are not, find out how to get back on target. If your target is still beyond reach, redefine it!

This system is designed to make full use of all the skills of every professional without fear or favour, and each is brought in to play his or her part.

DO NOT SEE THINGS AS THEY ARE AND SAY, 'WHY.'

SEE THINGS AS THEY COULD BE AND SAY, 'WHY NOT.'

Adam Smith

---

* if a policy is not age admitted it simply means that the insurance company have not seen the birth and marriage certificates (or a certified copy); a problem only arises when a claim is due, either on death or maturity. The insurance company will not pay out any proceeds until the age is proved. So why not do it now, and save yourself or your family a problem later?

3

WHY DO I NEED A FINANCIAL PLAN?

IT IS NOT ENOUGH TO HAVE A GOOD FINANCIAL PLAN
THE MAIN THING IS TO PUT IT INTO OPERATION

A fortune will flow through your hands during your working life. How much will you keep? (For a record of how much you will earn over your working life see Appendix iv).

A person aged twenty currently earning £8000 will, by the age of sixty-five, (assuming a 7 per cent increase in earnings) have earned the incredible sum of £1-1/4 million. How much will he or she have left?

What you will have to show for it will depend on your ability to manage and control your money.

In Britain most of us have the opportunity to work and earn money – the trouble is we just have not learned how to keep it.

The following figures have already been presented in a previous chapter, but I feel they need to be looked at several times for the size of the problem to be fully appreciated.

Here in the UK (1990), out of every 100 men now aged twenty-five, by age sixty-five:

One will be wealthy
Four will be rich
Sixteen will be self-supporting
Fifty-four will be dependent on the State, friends and relations
Twenty-five will be dead

Is there anyone who would not like to be in the top 5 per cent or at worst the top 21 per cent? To be there you need to plan – the sooner you start, the better your prospects are of being in that top 5 per cent.

People say, 'Things are getting better.' But are they? Look at the figures prepared ten years ago:

In the UK out of every 100 men now aged twenty-five, by age sixty-five (figures from 1980):
> One will be wealthy
> Four will be rich
> Sixteen will be self-supporting
> Forty-five will be dependent on the State and friends and relations
> Thirty-four will be dead

So all that has happened is that we have saved nine lives and made them dependent. This means people are living longer but not any better.

THERE ARE THREE MAIN PROBLEMS IN LIFE:

1. DYING TOO SOON AND LEAVING THE FAMILY IN POVERTY.
2. BECOMING DISABLED AND RELYING ON OTHERS.
3. LIVING TOO LONG AND ENDING UP IN POVERTY.

Once again, see how people living today have looked after themselves:

Over one-third of all senior citizens live below the poverty line; and 90 per cent of deaths after retirement have been traced to financial worries.

It has been estimated that in each home with the head of the household over age sixty-five:

66 per cent have an income of less than £99 per week.

Government pension and social security benefits are never adequate to fund a reasonable standard of living (never mind a comfortable one – they never were intended to provide anything but the very basics) in retirement, and the benefits look like diminishing even more in the future.

Remember that this is happening in one of the richest countries in world history.

Many battles have been fought in and out of court over the custody of a dependent child but how many battles have been fought over a dependent parent?

We have already noted the status of retired people today, after working a lifetime. We see here what happens in the event of the death or long term illness of the breadwinner.

A study of families who lost their breadwinner shows that the survivors' income dropped to 44 per cent of what they had been used to. Six out of ten family incomes immediately fell well below the amount needed to maintain an acceptable standard of living; nine out of ten families had serious financial problems within twelve months of the death of the breadwinner. The average family has enough life protection to provide an income for less than two years.

Widow's comment:

> 'I did not like it but one of the first things I had to set right was money.'

Life assurance is not about providing large sums of money. It is about providing a large tax-free sum to be invested, to provide future income (ideally inflation protected) for dependents for as long as they need financial support.

The figures for illness and disability should also be reiterated:

Over 2700 people start claiming sickness benefit each day.

Over 800,000 people have been sick or disabled and unable to work for over ten years.

YOU MUST PLAN AND PLAN NOW, TO AVOID LATER ECONOMIC HARDSHIP

Until recently, financial planning has been regarded as a service reserved for the wealthy. But today people at all income levels find themselves starting to realize the need for financial guidance; the trouble is where to go, and who to see when you get there.

the less affluent in our society now recognize their need for such planning because each £ of income means more to them.

QUESTIONS TO ASK YOURSELF

How long have you been working? How much have you earned? How much do you have left? How much longer will you be working? How much more will you earn? And how much will you then have left?

Would you like to be in the same position in ten years or would you like to be better off?

IT IS UP TO YOU WHAT YOU DO ABOUT IT

To start to plan is to start to be successful: you will never arrive if you do not start.

Take the challenge and grasp the opportunity whilst you have it.

Get your finances together and gain control over your money. Start to build your way to financial independence.

A strategy must be designed to ensure your success in personal financial planning and to make the most of what you have.

YOU SHOULD START BY:

Examining the reasons behind your financial behaviour. These could be:

Because ancestors suffered during the depression and other bad times who have passed on a basic fear of financial disaster and of spending, even to the extent of depriving themselves of a comfortable existence when it could be afforded.

We have been taught to make money from working and not by investing. All too often our financial goal is just a high salary. Surely it would be better if the goal changed to the provision of a higher standard of living for both now and in the future. After all, you worked hard to get your money, so you should make your money work hard for you.

The way we look at and handle money seems to be controlled by fear, and sometimes beliefs that have nothing to do with finance. Fortunately the most common fears are fairly easy to identify:

A fear of responsibility faced with a decision. We tend to hide from problems and hope they will go away; we prefer to ignore them rather than do something about them. What we need is someone to help define the problem and to assist us in making informed decisions. Many people tend to think that if they don't try they won't fail – yet the only true failure is actually the failure to try.

Just plain fear can also appear as a worry that by overspending today we might have nothing to spend tomorrow.

The fear of risk and not understanding the differences between saving and investing causes us to bury our heads in the sand. Yet this ostrich-like behaviour is a common sign, and it usually means that we are so worried about doing the wrong thing with our money that, at the end of the day, we do nothing. This total inactivity and inertia can literally cost a fortune in lost opportunities.

We should learn to set aside emotion where financial matters are concerned; this should enable us all to start the process of learning to control and manage our financial affairs more efficiently and more effectively.

When we have savings which we are afraid to invest, this usually stems from a lack of knowledge of, and a lack of trust in the financial industry and in our financial advisers. We will trust medical specialists with our lives, despite the majority of us being ignorant of medical practices, yet it does not always follow that we will trust financial specialists with our money.

The fear of money itself; we do not usually have much difficulty in adapting to a higher income but become frightened when presented with a large lump sum. There is an innate fear that once we start to manage money it will take control of, and start to manage us – remember Scrooge? Once we understand that we can keep our ideals and at the same time manage our finances more efficiently, we begin to treat handling money as a routine task (sometimes even pretending that it belongs to someone else).

THE CURE OF ALL THE ABOVE FEARS IS NOT DIFFICULT

KNOWLEDGE AND ACTION

To make it easier to take action, design a plan for sorting out your finances, getting them organized and making the most of what you have.

THE FIRST STEP TOWARDS GAINING CONTROL OF YOUR FINANCIAL LIFE IS TO DRAW UP A PERSONAL BALANCE SHEET OF WHAT YOU OWN AND WHAT YOU OWE.

Take a sheet of paper and list all your assets on one side and all your liabilities on the other side. Subtract one from the other and the answer is your net worth.

ASSETS	LIABILITIES
Total Assets £ A	Total Liabilities £ L

Net Worth = £ A - L

Your net worth will reveal your overall current financial position.

Now you know your net worth, set your goals. With help from your financial adviser, design a strategy to reach your goals.

Constantly monitor your progress and continually reassess your goals.

Budgeting is the simple process of keeping expenses in line

with income so that financial fear can be turned into financial fitness.

It may reveal that you can enjoy a few extra luxuries. It could also help you pinpoint the problems which you can then solve before they become too big to solve easily.

Usually the more money you have the less you can account for how you spend it.

Now take another sheet of paper and list all your outgoings on one side and your net income on the other. Deduct one from the other and you have your cash flow position.

INCOME	OUTGOINGS
Net Income £ I	Total Outgoings £ O

The Problem = £ I - O

By setting aside a short time each month over the next few months to consider your income and expenditure you should be able to:
1. Start to reduce any overspending and plan to build up a cash reserve for emergencies.
2. When you have achieved this, the next step is to include some form of saving and investing programme for the future.
3. Examine closely each month, exactly how much money comes in, and even more importantly, how much goes out. Look at your cash flow with a view towards adjusting your spending to match your financial plans.
4. Constantly check to see that your revised spending patterns are viable and adjust for any problem areas.
5. Develop a cash flow forecast by gathering your records of the past year. Include all items and start to keep full financial

records.

Use this forecast to estimate your outgoings for the next year and ensure that it is less than your income, for, as Mr Micawber said:

> 'Income twenty pounds outgoings nineteen and eleven pence, result happiness, but if outgoings twenty pounds and one penny, result misery.'

If you find that it does not balance and that your income is disappearing into that never never land called miscellaneous you have problems. If you are overspending find out where and take action.

It has been suggested that approximately 70 per cent of your income should be used for fixed expenses (rent, rates, mortgage, gas, food etc.); 15 per cent for various repairs (maintenance of clothing and home), and for entertainment and leisure; 10 per cent for insurance premiums; 5 per cent for savings. If you are a two income family then that should be 5 per cent each, but if your joint income exceeds £15,000 then fixed expenses should be less and you may be able to save around 10 per cent each.

You should continually evaluate your cash flow statement. Successful budgeting depends on being realistic; neither too rigid nor too loose. If you like to spend extra in some areas, do so – but make sure that you adjust in other areas.

Remember that you can ruin all your good intentions by being too tough with yourself or your spouse. A good budget should be positive – not negative. The purpose of this budget is to release cash to save for your future, but not at the total cost of today 'balance is everything'.

Your first goal should be a strategic reserve for financial emergencies. Aim to accumulate at least three months net income in an easily accessible account (Building Society or Bank) to protect against any financial emergency, for example, your car breaking down.

By doing this you will give your family an element of security. This will then enable you to devote your attention to saving for the future, secure in the knowledge that, if a problem occurs today, you are equipped to handle it.

Protection against personal risks: loss or damage to

property, loss of life, loss of health and/or loss of income, should also be considered at this initial stage.

The secret of successful saving is to do it with the same regularity that you pay your mortgage. Most people still tend to save by subtracting their other expenses from their income and trying to save from what is left (usually nothing).

Reverse the equation: set aside your savings first and pay your bills afterwards – in other words pay yourself for the future, first not last if at all. This should not be taken too literally, however, but savings should be an integral part of your budget and not purely an afterthought.

Consider using most or all of any pay rise for saving instead of increasing spending.

BUDGETING SHOULD BE A FAMILY AFFAIR WITH ALL MEMBERS INVOLVED

Even your children should be aware that everyone, including you, is operating within the framework of a budget. It could help them to be more prudent when they grow up.

Both parties should be involved with the record keeping, as well as the preparation of the budget – regardless of who is actually paying the bills. *Finances should always be joint decisions.*

If balancing your income and expenditure is to become a habit you need a budget that is both understood and easy to follow. Most people fail the battle of the budget because they take on too much too soon, become discouraged, and then give up.

You cannot manage to save 10 per cent of your earnings and at the same time pay off outstanding debts. If you generate a realistic budget, you know that you will reach your financial goal in due course, and your sense of well being and self esteem will soar.

When it is time to start to invest, decide on your financial objectives; a new home, private education, comfortable retirement, a wedding, or a better way to buy your home.

THE FINANCIAL PLANNING CYCLE

Determine where you are, where you want to be, how to get there, and constantly monitor progress – and be flexible. The sure way not to succeed is not to start planning.

There are many routes but once you know where you are, where you want to be and when you want to be there, your Adviser can set out a number of ways to enable you to reach your target. The route you choose will depend on *your* outlook, investment attitude, and ambitions, combined with your Adviser's input in offering best advice.

All the recommendations offered should be based on your own situation, wants, needs and desires, thus enabling you to make an informed decision.

Financial planning acts like a rudder controlling the direction of your financial life.

FINANCIAL PLANNING COVERS

investment attitude; family needs; asset accumulation; retirement needs; policy analysis; short, medium and long term goals; income and expenditure analysis; future income needs; money control; tax planning; house purchase; Wills and Trusts; protecting assets and income; managing your affairs; Executor and Trustee guidance; estate planning; business protection and portfolio management.

> THE LONGEST JOURNEY STARTS WITH A SINGLE STEP
> (Chinese Proverb)

4

WHAT WILL HAPPEN TO MY FAMILY WHEN I DIE?

> *'The most loving act a husband can do is to teach his wife how to be a widow'*
> Lynn Caine (widowed 1975)

THE PROBLEM:
DYING TOO SOON AND LEAVING YOUR FAMILY POOR

THE RESULT:
DEATH CREATES AN IMMEDIATE NEED FOR CASH

As I said in an earlier chapter:

Out of every 100 men aged twenty-five now, twenty-five will be dead before age sixty-five

Out of every 100 ladies aged twenty-five now, eleven will be dead before age sixty,

TODAY IN THE UK
OVER 700 PEOPLE WILL DIE
OVER 450 WIVES WILL BECOME WIDOWS
OVER 200 HUSBANDS WILL BECOME WIDOWERS

Six out of ten widows immediately have financial problems
Nine out of ten widows have financial problems after twelve months

Three out of four widows remarry for financial reasons.

The average homeowning family has the home paid for plus less than two years income in the event of the death of the breadwinner. If the family home is rented, then the problem is much worse because the rent still has to be paid.

QUESTIONS YOU MUST ASK YOURSELF

WHEN YOU DIE WOULD YOU WANT:
- *your widow to be your beneficiary*
- *your widow to have sufficient income to maintain her and your children's standard of living*
- *your widow to have to go out to work, leaving your children for others to look after in order to earn a living*
- *your widow to lower her and your childrens's standard of living*
- *your widow to have to sell the family home*
- *your widow to get married again for financial reasons eg. to keep the car or home, take the children on holiday, live comfortably*
- *your widow to wait six months for probate and then possibly discover that the only income she has is from less than 50 per cent of the estate, and is fixed for life.*

ARE YOU HAPPY FOR THE ABOVE TO HAPPEN TO YOUR WIDOW, TO YOUR FAMILY? IF SO, DO NOTHING

IF YOU DO NOT WANT THE ABOVE TO HAPPEN TO YOUR WIDOW OR TO YOUR FAMILY:
IS WHAT YOU HAVE DONE ENOUGH? COULD YOU DO MORE?

AFTER ALL, YOUR RESPONSIBILITIES TO YOUR FAMILY DO NOT END WITH YOUR DEATH

If you have not done anything, or what you have done is insufficient, you need to see your financial adviser today! TOMORROW MAY BE TOO LATE!

If you are having difficulty making ends meet, how much worse will it be for your family when you die?

Even if you do manage quite nicely now, how would your family fare if your income stopped?

It is not sufficient to say, *'The house will be paid for if I die.'*

If your mortgage was paid off today, could you afford to stop working? Surprisingly, that is what many breadwinners seem to expect their family to do, although they do not realize it themselves: they do not think in these terms, they are not told, it is not explained to them.

As I said earlier, *'You may have thirty years to plan for your retirement but you may not even have thirty minutes to plan for your death.'*

OFTEN LIFE ASSURANCE IS THE ONLY (OR THE MOST COST EFFICIENT AND TAX EFFICIENT) WAY OF PROVIDING THAT CASH.

WHAT YOU CAN DO:
YOU CAN SEE YOUR FINANCIAL ADVISER – NOW!

Arrange for a capital sum to provide your widow with sufficient income to ensure that she can bring up the children in the manner you would have, if you had lived.

DEATH DOES CREATE A NEED FOR CASH: EXAMPLE

John aged thirty-one, a clerk earning £10,000 pa., is married to Jean aged twenty-three, with a baby six months old. Jean has stopped work to bring up little James.

John is killed in a car accident going to work.

The only life assurance he had was two times his salary from work and mortgage protection.

After John's death, Jean still has all the household expenses, other than the mortgage repayments, so she has sufficient income to last (assuming 6 per cent inflation and 10 per cent capital growth) approximately two years, providing no major financial problem occurs.

What can she do?

Find a job? Not easy – especially one which fits in with child minders; however, both John and Jean wanted her to look after James, and she does not like the idea of a stranger, or even another member of the family, becoming James's mother as well as his father.

Sell the house? Not necessarily the answer – the proceeds of the sale would not enable her to pay rent and act as an income

for ever; she also likes where she lives.
   She would like to keep the car: can she afford it?
   She would like a holiday sometime: can she afford it?
   They had planned to send James
      to private school: can she afford it?

DID JOHN REALLY WANT JEAN AND JAMES TO HAVE THESE PROBLEMS?

I think not. He was just not warned. He just did not plan. He just did not realize.

So, on top of the emotional problems, Jean has serious financial worries – although John had as much protection as Mr Average, it was still nowhere near enough to do the job required.

WHAT JOHN'S FINANCIAL ADVISER COULD HAVE DONE FOR THEM

He could have insured his life to provide, in the event of John's death, a *tax free* capital sum sufficient to allow John's family to maintain their standard of living for as long as is necessary.

John had worked hard for his money: so his adviser should have made certain that John's foresight in providing extra capital for his family in the event of his death, would ensure that the extra money worked hard for his family when John could not.

For around £10* per month, John could have provided over £100,000 of additional life protection which, if invested together with the company protection, would have given Jean sufficient income to maintain her standard of living for around twenty years.

This would give her time: time to bring up James in the manner John would have liked, time to sort out her life, time to rebuild her life.

How would John have liked his family to remember him? As a loving person that cared for them enough to plan?

---

* do you realize it would take John over 833 years to pay as much into his life policy as Jean would receive (10 x 12 = 120; 100,000/120 = 833.33).

Or
as someone who loved them but did not have the foresight to plan?

Having said this, it was also up to Jean to take her part in the planning: perhaps I should have asked, 'Whose fault is it – John's, the Adviser's, or Jean's?'

WHAT ELSE COULD YOUR FINANCIAL ADVISER DO?

He could have arranged for protection on Jean's life. After all, if Jean had died, how would John have looked after little James? He would still have to work, to earn money.

He would need additional cash to help pay for someone to look after James whilst he was at work, to help with the washing, to help with the cooking, to help with the shopping and all the other myriad jobs that Jean used to do. He would not want little James effectively to lose his father as well as his mother.

WHAT ELSE CAN YOUR FINANCIAL ADVISER DO?

He or she could arrange for the level of protection to increase each year, in line with inflation, so that the actual value of the protection remains the same.

They can arrange that, if you are off ill, your premiums are paid by the insurance company, and they can also arrange for you to have a contingency day at least once a year: a day in which you review the events of last year and replan for next year.

It is essential, for both yourself and your family, that they help you to prepare a booklet outlining everything you have, where it is kept, what it is worth and who is to look after it. The booklet should list all your financial and policy details, all your advisers, in fact *every piece of information needed during life and after your death.*

Your adviser must help you to discuss everything with your family: your plans for your and your family's future if you live and when you die (remember, mortality is 100 per cent per person). As I have already said, you may have twenty, thirty or even forty years to plan for your retirement, but you may not even have thirty minutes to plan for your death, so:

SO, IF IT NEEDS TO BE DONE, DO IT AND DO IT NOW!

REMEMBER IF YOU DON'T DO IT YOUR FAMILY WILL BEAR THE COST

Planning for your death obviously will not benefit you, financially, but it WILL benefit and help your loved ones, financially and therefore emotionally. Believe me, I am not saying that money can replace you but it will make life much easier for your loved ones and ensure that your plans for them can continue.

It will enable them: to maintain their dignity, to remain in the family home as a family unit, to live the life you would wish them to and to remember you as a caring, loving person who thought of them before himself.

HOW DO YOU DECIDE THE LEVEL OF PROTECTION THAT YOU NEED?

With your adviser, decide the weekly (monthly, or annually, depending on how you normally plan) income that your family would need in the event of your death (taking into account that the mortgage would be paid). Decide on the number of years this income would be needed – ask your Financial Adviser the capital sum that would be needed to produce the required income, escalating at whatever rate you feel is appropriate, and then you can add anticipated funeral costs. This amount should be indexed and reassessed every year to take in the effect of inflation, changed circumstances and/or requirements.

The above is one answer; there are other ways of providing a solution, but again you need to see your Financial Adviser.

The cost is often much less than you think (around £10 per month in John's case); although you should not regard it as a cost but as an investment: an investment which will protect your family's future, give them financial security, and more selfishly, give you peace of mind now, and help them remember you with love.

I will now tell you of an actual, more complicated case which will show most successfully the effect of writing a Will and making use of Trusts, and the benefits that can and often do occur.

This particular client took over two years to come and see me after the initial recommendation, the reason being that he was very happy with his existing arrangements and Financial

Adviser.

I think you will see why he was glad that he eventually did come to me – although, in actual fact, what I did was relatively simple, the effect was very dramatic.

We arranged for a Will (using his own solicitor) to be drawn up: I then age admitted* his existing policies and placed several of them into Trust.

The next few pages show the difference my recommendations made:

---

* to age admit means to prove to the insurance company your date of birth – normally by production of your birth certificate. If age not admitted, no payments will be made by the insurance company either on death or maturity.

ESTATE VALUATION
(approximate on second death)
(before recommendation 1988/89)

Pension	(Mr – not in trust)	£ 10,725	
Pension	(Mr – in trust)	£	
Pension	(Mrs – not in trust)	£	
Pension	(Mrs – in trust)	£	
Life Assurance	(Mr – not in trust)	£110,000	
Life Assurance	(Mr – in trust)	£	
Life Assurance	(Mrs – not in trust)	£ 45,714	
Life Assurance	(Mrs - in trust)	£	
Life Assurance	(Mr - assigned)	£ 54,000	
Life Assurance	(JLSD - in trust)	£	

Total Life Assurance £220,439

House Value (approx)	£ 70,000
Business Value (approx)	£200,000
Assets (approx)	£ 20,000
Total Assets	£290,000

Total £510,439

Less Life Assurance (assigned) £ 54,000

Total Estate Value £456,439

Less
Business Relief	£100,000
Life Assurance (in trust)	£
Pension (in trust)	£
Total	£100,000

Total Taxable Estate £356,439

Inheritance Tax Liability

£ 0 – £110,000	Nil
£110,000 – £356,439 @ 40%	£ 98,576

Net Transfer   £357,863

Summary of the Current Inheritance Tax Situation
Inheritance Tax payable £98,576
Inheritance Tax payable as a percentage of the gross Estate 21.60%
No cash available until Probate granted
Surplus cash £67,863 (£220,439 - [£54,000 £98,576])

As there were other personal complications my estimate of the time for probate could have easily have taken two years. The same time scale and problems would have occurred if just the husband had died although the tax treatment would have been different. His wife (widow) would have been without any money until probate had been granted and this with three dependent children at school. Neither would she have been his main beneficiary.

ESTATE VALUATION
(approximate, on second death)
(initial recommendations 1988/89)

Pension	(Mr – not in trust)	£
Pension	(Mr – in trust)	£ 10,725
Pension	(Mrs – not in trust)	£
Pension	(Mrs – in trust)	£
Life Assurance	(Mr – not in trust)	£
Life Assurance	(Mr – in trust)	£110,000
Life Assurance	(Mrs – not in trust)	£
Life Assurance	(Mrs – in trust)	£ 45,714
Life Assurance	(Mr – assigned)	£ 54,000
Life Assurance	(JLSD – in trust)	£

Total Life Assurance   £220,439

House Value (approx)	£ 70,000
Business Value (approx)	£200,000
Assets (approx)	£ 20,000
Total Assets	£290,000

Total		£510,439
Less Life Assurance (assigned)	£ 54,000	
Total Gross Estate Value		£456,439
Less		
Business Relief	£100,000	
Life Assurance (in trust)	£155,714	
Pension (in trust)	£ 10,725	
Total	£266,439	
Total Taxable Estate		£190,000

Inheritance Tax Liability

£ 0 – £110,000	Nil	
£110,000 – £190,000 @ 40%	£ 32,000	
Net Transfer		£424,439

Effect of Initial Recommendation on the Potential Inheritance Tax due
Inheritance Tax payable as a percentage of the gross Estate
7.01%
£66,576 less Inheritance Tax paid (as a percentage of the Estate 14.58%)
Cash surplus £134,439 (£220,439 – [£54,000 £32,000])
£166,439 immediate Tax free transfer (Probate not needed)
Immediate Tax free cash (£166,439) would be available either to the spouse if just the client died, or to the children if both parents died. Also probate would have taken approximately three months instead of up to two years. This can be done for many people if only they would see a true Professional Financial Adviser.

Summary of the advantages:
   At least eighteen months saved in obtaining probate.
   £66,576 less potential liability to Inheritance Tax.
An immediate Tax Free transfer of £166,439 (instead of

nothing).
A tremendous reduction in the amount of aggravation for his beneficiaries.
Peace of mind now.

The cost? Well, he was happy with the fee, and felt it a small price to pay for all the above advantages.

I do feel that this is a particularly good example, which illustrates very clearly the advantages of effective tax and time planning.

Similar results can be achieved for many people if they see a Professional Financial Adviser.

YOU MUST ARRANGE TO SEE A SOLICITOR AND WRITE A WILL

Most husbands assume that their wives are their beneficiaries: many widows could have told them differently: because (according to the law of the land unless a valid Will states otherwise) their wives – sorry, widows – are not automatically their beneficiaries: a fact which many widows have found to their cost.

A Will, like Life Assurance, is one of the most unselfish things you can do, for it does not benefit you directly in a financial way (although it will give you great satisfaction to know that your wishes will come true), but it can certainly make life very simple for your beneficiaries and ensure that your wishes are carried out.

Again I say:

*IT IS THE HUSBAND'S RESPONSIBILITY TO ENSURE HIS FAMILY'S FINANCIAL WELL-BEING:
BOTH DURING HIS LIFE
AND AFTER HIS DEATH.*

5

WHAT WILL HAPPEN TO ME AND MY FAMILY IF I SUFFER LONG TERM ILLNESS?

WOULD YOUR INCOME COLLAPSE LIKE A PACK OF CARDS?

The financial and emotional impact of long term illness is often much worse than that of death. Good health, like your future income, cannot be taken for granted.

As Mr Micawber said:

> 'Annual income twenty pounds annual expenditure nineteen pounds nineteen shillings and sixpence: result happiness.'
> 'Annual income twenty pounds annual expenditure twenty pounds and sixpence: result misery.'

THE SIZE OF THE PROBLEM:
In 1982 33 per cent of men and 37 per cent of women reported long standing infirmity

EVERY DAY IN THE UK
Over 2700 people will start claiming sickness benefit
Over 850,000 will have been sick or disabled for over one year
Over 100,000 people will have been sick or disabled and unable to work for over ten years

WILL YOU BE ONE OF THEM?

What would happen to you and to your family if you suffered long-term disablement? What would happen to your standard of living? Would it collapse like a house of cards?
Who would pay the bills?
Could you remain in your home?
What would happen to your children?
Could you afford: to keep your car? to take holidays? to live comfortably?

Do you like the idea of the above happening? Would you like to do something about it? Are you going to do something about it? Or are you willing to take the chance that it will not happen to you?

Remember – it will happen to over 2700 people today, tomorrow and the day after.

Can you take the chance that it is not you and your family heading for financial and emotional disaster?

I took that chance and it did happen to me.

I was not aware. I did not think. I did not plan, and as a result I lost my health, my wealth and fourteen years of my life and my family's lives. I could have protected myself and my family but I did not, and in saving just a few pounds, I lost thousands.

I have recently gained a new client who, several years previously, had agreed to buy life, medical and income protection from an adviser. However, his accountant said, 'Leave it for two months and start the payments in your new financial year.'

Two days before his new financial year he had a heart attack.

He, like me, survived – but he lost his living (a large retail carpet business) and scraped by in poverty for several years, before he started to regain his health and was able to find a low paid position.

The moral is:

IF YOU DECIDE TO DO IT . . . DO IT NOW

DON'T WAIT FOR TOMORROW. IT MIGHT BE TOO LATE!

No doubt you are aware of private hospital treatment, but did you know that *you can arrange for your income not only to continue, but to increase each year in line with average earnings, until retirement.*

Have you realized that you can arrange for your pension contributions not only to be paid, *but to be paid on an increasing basis, until retirement (ie your pension could be unaffected by your inability to pay for it through injury or illness).*

Have you been told that *it can be arranged for you to receive a large tax free lump sum on the diagnosis of many of the major diseases.* This cash would help to pay for any extras needed ie. modifications to the home or car.

I often arrange the above when clients buy a home. We treat a mortgage as a full financial and tax planning exercise; after all, it is probably the most expensive purchase in your lifetime and should therefore be treated as an integral part of all financial planning, instead of just an ad hoc purchase, such as a new coat.

New clients are usually surprised at the care and thought that goes into the process, and how little extra these necessary benefits cost – however, as I said earlier, I do not regard them as a cost but rather as an investment – an investment in your and your family's future.

This extra investment varies with age but is usually around the equivalent of ¼ per cent or ½ per cent extra.

Most people I meet are very happy to know that if they were off work through illness, they would receive up to 75 per cent of their income, and that they would not have to pay either the endowment or the interest payment after an initial period of three months.

The financial and emotional impact of long term disability is often many times worse than the financial and emotional impact of death.

I can assure you I know, I have been there.

Are YOU prepared?
if not
what can you do?

SEE YOUR FINANCIAL ADVISER

WHAT CAN HE OR SHE DO FOR YOU?

With your help to quantify the problem he or she can bundle it up, put it in his or her briefcase and take it away with them.

WHO WILL TAKE CARE OF YOU AND YOUR FAMILY WHEN YOU CANNOT?

6

WHAT WILL HAPPEN TO ME IF I LIVE TO RETIREMENT?

ARE YOU ON COURSE FOR POVERTY?

The Problem:
Living too long and ending up in poverty.
Look at the figures again:

FACT
85 out of every 100 people aged seventy-five do not have £150 of spendable cash

FACT
90 out of 100 deaths after age sixty-five are partially caused by financial worries

FACT
One third of all senior citizens live below the poverty line

FACT
With the head of the household age sixty-five or over:
66 per cent have an income of less than £99 per week

FACT
In 1967 £1000 was worth £1000:
By 1977 it was worth £644
By 1987 it was worth £180
By 1997 it will be worth ?p

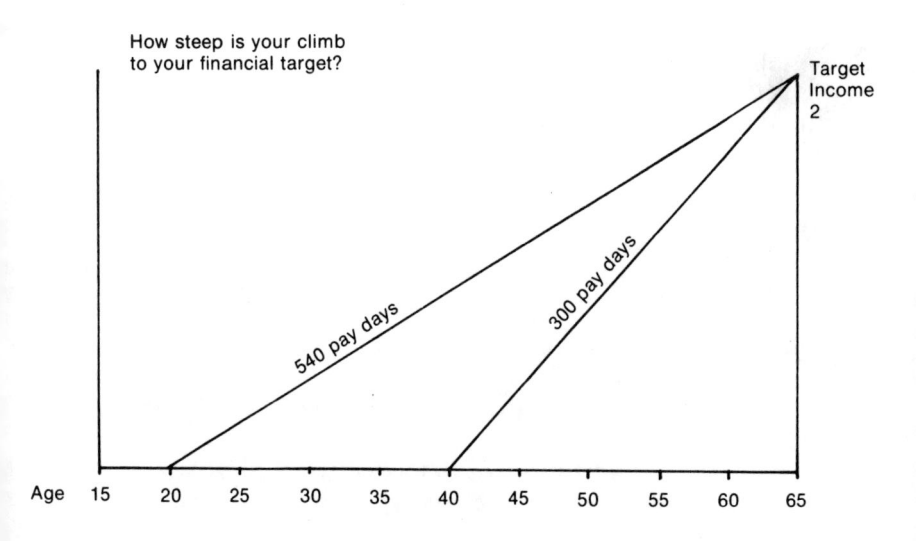

How steep is your climb to your financial target?

Graph showing two lines rising to Target Income 2 at age 65: one starting at age 20 labelled "540 pay days", another starting at age 40 labelled "300 pay days".

FACT
It is no longer a question of how much money do you have but rather of how much it is worth

FACT
Out of every 100 men age twenty-five now, by age sixty-five:

One will be wealthy
Four will be well to do
Sixteen will be self supporting

Fifty-four will be dependent upon the State and or relatives

Which section of the above do you wish to be in?

If you wish to be in the top 21 per cent you must plan now:
The longer you wait, the higher the cost, the steeper the climb, the lower the return, the harder the journey, the poorer your future.

Today in the UK we have the ability to earn a substantial sum of money. A person aged thirty now earning £12,000 pa will, by age sixty, have earned a total of £1,240,793. The trouble is that, as yet, we have not learned how to keep our money and make it work for us. This is mainly due to a lack of realization of the fact that 'our future is in our own hands, and if we do not plan and sow, we will not receive'. A high salary tends to be our main aim in life, and we pay little or no attention to the accumulation and growth of our capital; ironically, it will be that accumulated capital that will look after us in our retirement.

We have a tendency to leave the planning to the State or to our employer, but although it is true that they do have a part to play in our welfare, we must be responsible for our own future. How can we make our money grow and work hard for us in real terms?

Consider yet again how people living today have looked after themselves.

It is useless, and indeed, defeatist, to think that:

'It's a struggle to manage well enough today, someone will look after me in the future.'

Just look again at the figures.

That 'someone' will not be there unless you plan for them to be there now, and then that 'someone' will be yourself.

There is a saying in our industry:

'Would you give your old dad a tenner a week?'

Of course you would!

You will be old one day, so why not give yourself that 'tenner a week' now? There will then be no need for you to rely on your son or daughter for that 'little extra' which makes life bearable.

In other words, invest for your own future now. The sooner you start, the better your future – and the less it will cost you.

RISK! What is risk?

Risk is the difference between saving and investing.

If you save in 'safe' deposits, then history has proved that the real value of your money has always dropped over the long term, although the face value has steadily increased.

Spread stock market investments can (sorry not can, will) fall, as well as rise, on a day to day basis (even month to month or in very bad times year to year) but over the longer term history has proved that this type of investment has always increased the actual value of investments in real terms.

WHICH ROUTE CARRIES THE GREATER RISK?
Deposit
   Has no risk to face value, but a risk to actual value over the long term.

Pooled Investments
   Has a risk to the face value in the short term, but a good chance of an increase in actual value in the long term.

   Look now at the comparative growth both in face value and actual value of the average building society, compared with the average of the stock market from 1945 to 1991.

   If you had invested £100 on 31 December 1945, both in a building society and in the stock market, by 31 December 1990 the average return would have been:

	Building Society	Stock Market
Face Value	£ 899	£ 10,882
Actual Value*	£ 51	£ 622

   This means that both areas have their part to play in any financial plan, to achieve a reasonable balance of security and growth potential.

   Remember – advice must always be sought from a professional!

QUESTIONS THAT YOU MUST ASK YOURSELF

   How much of your capital do you want access to?
How much of your capital do you need for emergencies?

   If you live to retirement:
   Would you want to be able to afford – to live comfortably without financial worries, have a car, holidays when and where you wish, to keep up any hobbies, to 'treat' the grandchildren, to live in the area of your choice, to live without counting the pennies too closely, to enjoy life, to have an income indexed at least in line with the cost of living . . .?

---

* the spending power of the money at 1945 prices (Figures prepared by Barclays de Zoete Wedd)

If the answer to the above is 'yes', then you will have to do something about it – *and do it now.*

In order to do this, you will have to make the money for which you worked so hard, work hard for you. THE HARDER YOU MAKE IT WORK THE BETTER IT WILL LOOK AFTER YOU.

You need to start planning now. It is never too soon to plan for the future. If you do not plan, you will not succeed in achieving a financially secure retirement. Nothing worthwhile is achieved without planning, effort, thought and sacrifice.

Don't say, 'I can't do it,' because you never will. If you say, 'I can do it,' you might, but say, 'I will do it,' and you will.

Define each target and tackle them one at a time. A mountaineer might say, 'I want to climb that mountain range.' Unless he sits down, plans each mountain one by one, and decides on the order in which he is to climb them, he probably won't. With a methodical approach, he is then able to say, 'I will climb those mountains in this order' and the task is altogether less daunting.

It is just the same with financial planning.

THE MESSAGE IS: YOU MUST LOOK AFTER YOURSELF
– BECAUSE NO ONE ELSE WILL

You will not achieve your goals in one fell swoop, so decide in which order and to what extent you wish to tackle each goal and set out YOUR priorities.

Along the lines of *Spratt's Guide to Financial Recording and Planning,* prepare written details of your current financial position, your future financial goals and the route you need to take, together with all the information needed by you to maintain your goals, to reassess them, and also important, the information needed by your professional advisers, executors, trustees and guardians in the event of your premature death.

What you should seek to do is to look after yourself when you reach retirement, but also look after your loved ones if you don't make it to retirement.

HOW DO YOU DO IT?

By investing in yourself NOW! By planning for your future

NOW!

Example 1:
Fred did not believe in pensions: 'it was the State's job' to look after him when he retired.
Result: the old age pension, plus related earnings.
Fred's last monthly pay packet before he retired was £1200.
Fred's first monthly pay packet after he retired was £500.
Did Fred enjoy a drop of £700 per month in his income?

Example 2:
John believed in pensions, but not until he was forty, when he invested £40 a month with no increases.
John's last pay packet before he retired was also £1200.
John's first pay packet after he retired was £1100.
Plus a once only tax-free lump sum of nearly £21,000.

Example 3:
Sid started a pension of £20 when he was twenty.
Sid's last pay packet before he retired was also £1200.
Sid's first pay packet after he retired was £1500.
Plus a once only tax-free lump sum of nearly £35,000.

Who was happiest?

Of course, there are many other ways of planning for your financial future; however, it is not the object of this book to tell you how to plan in detail, but to show you the benefits of planning and the penalties of not planning.

Are you on course for poverty?
IF SO
You must contact your Financial Adviser for detailed planning.

WHAT SHOULD YOUR FINANCIAL ADVISER DO?
They should help you decide: what you want for yourself in the future, how to achieve your goals, and the cost of

achieving those goals.

A specific plan should be formed and written down, taking into account the above, and a financial commitment made. This financial commitment might be too small at the start, but providing that your plans are realistic, both in time and requirements, any shortfall should be recoverable in the future.

However, for some people it will be too late, because there will just not be enough time. For these all I can say is, something extra is better than nothing – but you can save your children or friends from making the same mistake.

Let us all do our best to remove the bottom 54 per cent; it can be done if we all plan and act – and let us hope it will be done.

FIGURES FOR A PERSONAL PENSION
(assuming 12 per cent growth)

For a Gross investment of £1 per day now
(net 75p std rate 60p HRT)

Age next at start	Pension paid at age 65
25	£146 per day
30	£ 80
35	£ 44
40	£ 24
45	£ 13
50	£ 7

COST OF ONE YEAR'S DELAY

AGE	GROSS CONT	TAX RATE 25%	NET CONT	FUND VALUE	SAVING	LOSS OVER RETIREMENT			
						FUND	CASH	PEN	TOTAL LOSS
									If Mr Average
29	500 pa	25	375	255,183					
30	500	25	375	227,572	375	27,611	8494	2523	43,816

AGE	GROSS CONT	TAX RATE 25%	NET CONT	FUND VALUE	SAVING	LOSS OVER RETIREMENT			
						FUND	CASH	PEN	TOTAL LOSS
									If Mr Average
34	750	25	563	215,417					
35	750	25	563	191,855	563	23,562	7249	2153	37,391

WILL YOU LIVE, FINANCIALLY, HAPPY EVER AFTER?

7

HOW DO I MAKE THE MOST OF MY INVESTMENTS?

To achieve above average results you must adopt above average means

> 'The chance of gain is often overvalued. The chance of loss is often undervalued.'
> Adam Smith

We all want to ensure that our savings are achieving good results, and that they are going to maintain and provide a 'real' increase in purchasing power in the years to come. But the investment market and the range of options available can be confusing. We will be looking at the investment choice open to us – banks, building societies, National Savings, stocks and shares, government securities, unit trusts and insurance policies. How do *you* decide on the most suitable method for your particular situation?

Objectives:
* Achieve above average growth
* Increase in actual value
* Flexibility in investment spread
* Provide extra income

The method chosen will very much depend on what you are

hoping to achieve. For example, are you investing for capital growth, or do you have a more immediate need for additional income? These are decisions which will have to be taken before any money is invested.

We will try to clarify some of these points so that you are better equipped to analyse the options available. Of course, we cannot cover every single angle of investment opportunity, but some of the ideas might open up some new avenues of thought for you.

WHAT DO YOU LOOK AT FIRST?
 * Short, medium or long term commitments?
 * Access to the capital?
 * What level and type of risk are you prepared to take?

Firstly you must ask yourself some simple questions. Bearing in mind that you must always keep some cash handy for a rainy day or for short term commitments:

Do you want an income from your investments? If so, when?
Are you more interested in capital growth? For future income?
Or a combination of both income and capital growth?

Are you likely to need the money on a specific date or are you investing for an indefinite period? Obviously, the longer it is invested then the greater the chance of a higher return.

Ask yourself what level and type of investment risk you are prepared to take. You have a broad range of options to choose from with varying degrees of risk attached to them.

At one end of the spectrum, you have the absolutely safe face value investments, such as banks and building societies; at the other end, you have the speculative investments – commodity futures, currencies, etc. with their great potential for a real gain as well as an actual loss.

FACE VALUE SECURITY	Banks, Building Societies National Savings
MEDIUM RISK TO FACE VALUE	Insurance Bonds, Unit Trusts Investment Trusts, Property
HIGHER RISK TO FACE VALUE	Stocks and Shares, Unlisted Securities
HIGH RISK TO FACE VALUE	Commodities & Futures, 3.30 at Haydock!

The problem that faces you as an investor is that potentially, much higher rewards are obtainable from those investments where there is an element of risk involved... however, the risk is that of actually losing money.

The amount of risk you are prepared to take usually depends on how much capital you have available for investment. You will not want to risk all your money in speculation. If you are lucky enough to have the financial resources to be able to invest some of your money in these different markets, then, with the benefit of professional investment advice, you should be able to achieve substantial returns.

Basic decisions to be made:
* What am I investing for?
* How much risk am I willing to take?

Here, it is important that we discuss the word 'risk'.

Deposit based investments have a guarantee of no loss in face value – but history has shown that, over the long term, deposit type savings have actually lost value ie. if you had invested £100 in January 1945 into the normal Building Society account, by December of 1990 the actual spending value would have been reduced to £51 (this is sometimes called the safest way to lose value).

Equity based investments, on the other hand, have no guarantee as to the face value, but history has shown that, over the longer term, the actual spending value has always increased ie. if £100 had been invested in the average of the Equities in January 1945, by December 1987 its actual value would have been £622 (this figure takes into account the crashes of 1973/74 and 1987).

So what is meant by the word *'risk'* I will leave each of you to decide.

For each different type of investment you must consider your tax position – your liabilities will vary according to whether you are a non tax payer, basic rate taxpayer or a higher rate taxpayer. Also consider how each type of investment is treated for Capital Gains Tax and Inheritance Tax purposes.

So far we have been considering mainly lump sum investments. You may wish to save on a regular basis towards say, retirement, school fees or a wedding. It might suit you better to discipline yourself by making a regular commitment so that you can be more confident of achieving your financial target.

The golden rule is 'do not put all your eggs in one basket'. Spread your investment in a variety of areas so that you are not dependent on the performance in one particular area or company, but do remember to review your investment regularly, as conditions are changing all the time.

Protecting your investment against inflation is one of the major problems which you should expect to face when selecting an investment medium. As we all know, inflation can rapidly begin to erode the value of our investments. It can greatly reduce our spending power. For example, even with inflation running at 5 per cent, the value of money will halve every fourteen and a half years.

You can see below the effect of inflation on the value of £1000:

Time	Inflation at 5%	10%
After 3 years	£858	£729
After 5 years	£774	£590
After 10 years	£598	£348

What are the most common investment options available? Well, the most obvious choice most people think of is Capital Protected or Deposit variety – for example, Building Society Share Accounts, Bank Deposit Accounts or National Savings.

1. Capital Protected Investment

With this type of investment the interest is paid on a regular basis, at a rate which is determined by the financial institution concerned. This can either be fixed at the outset for a specific term, or varied according to market conditions by the savings institution.

a) Building Societies

By far the most popular choice of saving for the general public is the ordinary share account. The great attraction for savers is accessibility: you can lay your hands on your money whenever you want. But you could expect to receive a slightly higher return if you place your money in an account where longer notices of withdrawal are required, or if you leave your money invested for a set period.

The advantage of this type of investment is that it is very convenient, because there are a large number of outlets up and down the high street. The face value of your investment is safe. But the price to be paid for this 'security' is that the return on your investment is unlikely to be spectacular or to provide 'real' growth.

All interest, prior to April 1991, credited by a building society was paid net of basic rate tax. This was done automatically by the building society before the interest was credited to your account and still is for taxpayers. However, if you are a non-taxpayer you can arrange for the building society to pay your interest gross. A note of warning here, as both men and women now have to complete their own tax return it is possible that if you become a taxpayer during the year you will have to repay the tax credited to your building society account.

For those paying tax at above basic rate, the effective return from building societies diminishes as the difference between basic rate and higher rate tax has to be paid in the form of a reduced tax allowance.

A new development is a Unit Trust that invests only in higher rate Building Society accounts. There are two advantages to this:
(i) Your investment will always be with the highest interest rate

available;
(ii) Non-taxpayers CAN reclaim the tax paid.

Of course the Unit Trust group will charge an initial investment fee and a management fee so this must be taken into account before any investment is made.

TESSA

From 1 January 1991 it has been possible for tax and non-taxpayers alike to invest up to £9000 over five years into a bank or building society account and, providing not a penny of the capital investment has been withdrawn within the five years, to have the tax paid on the interest re-credited to the account.

Offshore Account

Both banks and building societies have accounts held offshore that credit all interest gross although the interest does have to be declared and tax paid through your tax return it does have a slight grossing up effect.

Distributor Status

Several accounts are legally allowed to 'Roll Up' the interest gross and tax is only payable when the interest is actually withdrawn. This can be especially useful to higher rate taxpayers who can defer any liability until they are standard rate or even non-taxpayers.

b) Banks

A deposit interest cheque account with a high street bank is also a method of investment which will allow you easy access to your money, but at the same time it has the same advantages and drawbacks which are associated with the building societies.

The difference between banks and building societies is now very little, in fact one building society has already changed its status to that of a bank.

c) National Savings

Basically, National Savings is a system operated by the government to raise money from the public to help meet its borrowing requirements. There are various forms of savings available through the Post Office.

(i) National Savings Certificates: these are sold in units of £25, up to a maximum holding of £5000. The interest rate is fixed and guaranteed, whatever happens to other interest rates. The major advantage is that they are free from income tax and capital gains tax, therefore it is a very useful option for both the non-taxpayer and the higher rate taxpayer. A point to note about Savings Certificates is that the returns are not only tax free, but they also do not have to be entered on the annual returns to the Inland Revenue. This can make them a boon to the wife who wants to retain some investment of her own but wishes to avoid the problem of having the profits included on her tax form. However, rarely is there a silver lining without a cloud and in this case, the cloud is that you have to hold the certificates for five years to receive the best return.

(ii) Index Linked National Savings Certificates – the forerunner to these was the 'Granny Bond', because they were only available to the elderly. With subsequent issues this restriction has been removed. They are designed to guarantee your savings against inflation. The value is increased in line with the movement in the Retail Prices Index. An additional supplement is added to the value of the certificates if they are kept for the full term. The proceeds again are tax free.

Because the returns are linked to the RPI, it is a good way of protecting the value of your investments when inflation is high. When inflation is low it may be wiser to consider other forms of investment in order to achieve a more competitive return. As the investment is linked to the RPI, there can be no capital growth in 'real' terms.

(iii) Monthly Income Bonds and National Savings Deposit Bonds – these two different types of investment are designed for those people with a lump sum to invest – which they can afford (or think they can) to tie up for a long period of time in order to draw off an income. Again, no income tax is deducted before payment, but the proceeds are liable to tax and must be declared.

(iv) As well as these forms of savings, National Savings Investment Accounts which have a minimum deposit of £5 and a maximum of £50,000 are usually suited for the smaller saver with no tax liability. The interest rate is normally high, but since it is only credited once a year, on 31 December, the account lacks the compounding element that applies to banks and building society accounts, where interest is credited half-yearly or quarterly.

However, you do have the ease of access associated with a bank account, and the advantage of not paying tax automatically on the interest earned.

Banks, building societies and National Savings are examples of the type of investment whereby the financial institution sets the rate of return at the outset.

SOMETHING TO THINK ABOUT: Where do the banks and building societies invest your money?

2. Property

If you are a homeowner you will already be aware of the growth potential that property offers. However, in order to invest in industrial or commercial property you would require large sums of money and this usually prevents the individual investor from venturing into this particular market. This need not be 'the be all and end all', for you can invest in a property fund run by an insurance company, which offers the additional advantage of a collective investment. I will go into that later on.

3. British Government Stocks (GILTS)

Government Stocks or 'Gilts' are one of the most popular of the interest bearing investments. Gilts represent borrowing by the Government or certain nationalized industries which are guaranteed by the Government. If you invest in Gilts you can be sure that interest will be paid to you as the 'lender' and the principal repaid to you in accordance with the terms of the loan. A number of names are used for specific stocks eg. Treasury, Exchequer, Funding, Transport etc, but these have no real significance to the investor.

Gilts carry a fixed interest rate which is expressed as an annual rate on £100 nominal of the stock. For example, if you were to buy £100 nominal of Treasury 8.75 per cent 1997, you would receive £8.75 pa until 1997, subject to the deduction of basic rate income tax; and you will receive that amount irrespective of the price you have paid for the stock or the fluctuating price of the stock while you hold it. Wealth warning: the capital value can and probably will be eroded over the medium to long term.

In addition to the interest, the Government has the obligation to redeem the stock ie. repay each loan at the nominal value of £100. The nature of this obligation varies from stock to stock; it can be either to repay on a fixed date eg. Treasury 8.75 per cent 1997 to be redeemed on 1.9.97; or within a range of dates eg. British Gas 3 per cent 90/95 to be redeemed some time between 1.5.90 and 1.5.95. The period still unexpired before the redemption date is used to classify stocks as follows:

SHORTS   less than five years to redemption
MEDIUMS   between five and fifteen years to redemption
LONGS   over fifteen years to redemption

Interest is paid net of basic rate tax unless the stock is bought through the Post Office. Interest received is treated as investment income and is subject to higher rate tax where appropriate. However, if the stock is held for more than twelve months any gain is free from Capital Gains Tax.

4. Shares

Ordinary shares, or equities as they are more commonly termed, are a company's risk capital; the investor who buys them expects a reasonable and a rising level of dividend income and also a rise in the share price but there is no guarantee of either. Dividends are paid out of the company profits, normally following the recommendation of the directors. The market price will vary from day to day depending on past records of the company's profits, dividends and assets. The price will also be affected by subjective judgments on the company's future performance, news concerning the sector in which the company operates and the news affecting the economy as a whole.

Taxation – ordinary shareholders in receipt of dividend

income also receive a tax credit; non-taxpayers can reclaim payment of this tax credit. Whilst the liability for basic rate tax is satisfied by the credit, higher rate taxpayers will still have a liability. Any profit may be liable to Capital Gains Tax.

In addition, the investor must remember that the adviser will require commission on any transaction in which he is involved and, if he is managing a portfolio of shares for you, he will also charge a management fee. To minimize the risk factor it is necessary to hold a wide spread of investments throughout the various areas of the market.

It is the risk element which separates equities from capital protected investments ie. Banks.

When you take a risk with your capital you expect a higher than average return and, historically, this has been the case.

British Telecom gave many people the chance to invest in shares for the first time. Some, flushed with first success have tried their luck with more recent issues: Abbey Life, TSB, Water, Electricity etc.

It has been seen that the profits made on equities can and do far outstrip the more traditional forms of saving. Put simply, this is the difference between saving and investing.

BUT WHAT ABOUT THE RISK?

Isn't there a chance that you might lose your money?

The answer is 'yes'. There is always a risk in holding shares, and without the benefit of professional advice from a stockbroker or other adviser, it would be inadvisable for the individual to plunge into share ownership. Although there is nothing to stop you managing your own portfolio it is no easy matter, and if it is to be done properly it is extremely time consuming. There is a way round this, however, and this leads us to the advantages associated with unitized investment, whereby you pool your assets with others and reduce your risk by the widespread use of this type of investment. The investment decisions are taken for you by professional investment managers.

5 Unitized Investment

This can be done in three ways: by investment in a Unit Trust, in an Investment Trust, or by investment with an insurance company.

a) Unit Trusts

A unit trust is a means by which a group of individuals can pool their money together to form a larger fund. This is then invested on their behalf by professional investment managers. The actual funds are controlled by Trustees, who must be an independent body who will ensure that the Trust is managed in accordance with the Trust Deed. So, Unit Trusts can give you an opportunity to participate in the activities of the stock market with its potential for capital growth of direct investments, without having to spend the time and money acquiring the specialist expertize necessary to do so on your own. There are a bewildering number of trusts available (over 900) and they are invested in different sectors of the market. Again, it would be advisable to take professional advice before investing. The special tax position of Unit Trusts means that any income taken will be paid net of basic rate tax.

This means that for a basic rate taxpayer there will be no further tax to pay. The non-taxpayer will be able to reclaim, from the Revenue, the tax paid. This obviously has a big advantage over a bank or building society. A liability still remains for the higher rate taxpayer however. The Trust itself is not liable to Capital Gains Tax, therefore any payments under the trust to you will be liable to CGT – but as you have an annual exemption, the total gain has to be more than this before you have any actual liability. Advantage can also be taken of indexation.

b) Personal Equity Plans

These allow an individual over the age of eighteen to invest up to a certain amount (£3000 1990/91) into UK ordinary shares, and a further amount (£3000 1990/91) into unit trusts, and benefit from income tax relief on dividends paid and exemption from CGT on disposal

c) Life Assurance Bond

By investing into a single premium bond with an insurance company the individual investor once again has the advantages associated with unitized investment. The bond is also able to invest in a wider range of investments, including areas not available to unit trusts, and you are able to invest in various funds specializing in different sectors of the market ie. Property, Equity, Cash, Building Society, International etc. Most companies offer a Managed Fund (simply a bit of each) which is actively managed by their own experts. It is also possible to switch from fund to fund for a nominal charge as many times as you like (the first switch is usually free in any one year). Whilst the fund itself is liable to tax, there is no personal liability to basic rate tax on any income taken and the potential liability to higher rate tax can often be removed by 'top-slicing'. Another feature is that all taxpayers (including higher rate taxpayers) can take a 5 per cent income with no immediate liability to income tax. Care must still be taken on any withdrawal over 5 per cent as this can turn a standard rate taxpayer into a higher rate taxpayer and cause problems for those claiming full or marginal Age allowance.

There is no personal liability to Capital Gains Tax (this has already been allowed for in the unit price).

d) Investment Trusts

A British company listed on the stock exchange in which you buy shares rather than units, but which otherwise operates in a similar manner to Unit Trusts. Although not so well known, investment trusts have actually been around for much longer and their investment record is at least as good as Unit Trusts.

e) Regular Savings Plan

It is possible to invest into the unitized type funds on a regular monthly or annual basis, to save for future requirements in one of the most tax efficient ways possible, as proceeds can be TAX FREE (even at the higher rate). The typical mortgage endowment is a good example of this type of plan; they are also often used in school fees planning.

Independent Taxation

From April 1990, advice should be sought on the effect of this very sensible change on the taxation system, and therefore in whose name investments are registered. However a useful starting point is to consider the following questions:

* Where should our investments be placed?
* In whose name should they be registered?
* What effect will the new system have on our financial planning?

Example: (tax year 1990–1991)

John is sixty-eight, has a pension of £9500, and an investment income of £5000 pa. His wife, Jane is sixty-seven and has a pension of £500 pa. Before the next tax year, John will transfer sufficient investments to provide an income for Jane of £3000 pa. Assuming State pensions remain the same, the effect of this transfer is:

	1989/90 John	1989/90 Jane	1990/91 John	1990/91 Jane
Income				
Pension: State	£ 3,630	Nil	£ 2,267	£ 1,363
Company	£ 5,870	£ 500	£ 5,870	£ 500
Investment	£ 5,000	Nil	£ 2,000	£ 3,000
	£14,500	£ 500	£10,137	£ 4,863
Less Allowances				
Married Man's	£ 4,375	N/A	N/A	N/A
Wife's Earned	N/A	£ 500	N/A	N/A
Personal Age	N/A	N/A	£ 3,400	£ 3,400
Married Age	N/A	N/A	£ 1,985	N/A
Taxable Income	£10,125	Nil	£ 4,752	£ 1,463

	1989/90		1990/91	
	John	Jane	John	Jane
Income Tax Payable	£ 2,531	Nil	£ 1,188	£ 366
Net Income	£11,969	£ 500	£ 8,949	£ 4,497
Joint Net Income	£12,469		£13,446	

The Age Allowance Trap (tax year 1990–1991)

For most people, higher rate tax does not raise its ugly head until taxable income reaches £20,700 pa. (1990/91). But for some people, this loss of income to the taxman can start at around half that level.

Where your money is invested can have a great effect on the income of sixty-five year olds and it is possible for them to pay the equivalent of 60 per cent tax when the maximum level is supposed to be 40 per cent.

This is a complex area that is beyond the scope of this book but I would advise anyone age sixty or even less to give this a thought, so to prevent you falling into the 'age allowance trap' (and lose your allowance at the rate of £1 a year for every £2 of income) see your Professional Financial Adviser or Accountant.

DO YOU WANT TO BE A SAVER OR AN INVESTOR?

8

WHO WILL INHERIT MY ASSETS WHEN I DIE?

IF YOU DO NOT HAVE A WILL, WILL YOU REST IN PEACE?

DYING WITHOUT A VALID WILL

If you do not make a Will, the government will make one for you. Their Will is called Intestacy.

WOULD YOU REST IN PEACE?

Do you like the idea of the government writing YOUR Will (only they do not call it a Will they call it Intestacy) and deciding what happens to YOUR family and to YOUR assets?

More people commit intestacy than adultery but only because they do not realize the problems they leave behind.

WHERE THERE IS NO WILL THERE IS NO WAY THAT WHAT YOU WISH TO HAPPEN WILL HAPPEN

Do you want to decide what happens to everything you have built up in your lifetime, or would you prefer the government to do it for you?

Do you want

THE TAX MAN   THE COURTS   A STRANGER
    OR THE PERSON OF YOUR CHOICE

To carry out YOUR wishes?

I cannot stress enough the importance of seeing a solicitor, IMMEDIATELY, and writing your Will (DO NOT EVEN WAIT TO FINISH READING THIS BOOK).

If you die without a Will leaving a widow and children, the following WILL happen because:

The rules of Intestacy then apply. If we assume that the taxable estate is £200,000 then the amount of tax payable is a staggering 40 per cent – £80,000.

Your widow only has a right to the income (life interest) from half of the estate. To protect the children it has to be on deposit. The reason for this is that the value must never fall. This means that the best return she can hope for, in the long term, is an average of around 5 per cent. Your widow's income is effectively fixed for the rest of her life (what will be the value of that income, say, in forty years – a woman aged forty now has around forty-two years to live if she is Mrs Average).

If a Will has been written your assets would go just where you want them to. If, as is usually the case, you had willed everything to your widow, the estate would not have paid any Inheritance Tax.

SUMMARY

	INTESTATE ESTATE IS TAXABLE	WILL WRITTEN ESTATE IS NOT TAXABLE
ESTATE	£200,000	£200,000
TAX PAID	£ 80,000	NIL
NET TRANSFER	£120,000	£200,000

A SIMPLE WILL AND/OR THE USE OF A TRUST CAN PREVENT THIS AND ENSURE THAT YOUR WIDOW DOES NOT HAVE TO SUFFER THE ABOVE, AND WHAT YOU WISH TO HAPPEN WILL HAPPEN

ESTATE DISTRIBUTION
FLOW CHART OF THE RULES OF INTESTACY

IS THERE A VALID WILL?

Yes------------------------No

Estate divided as per Will   Rules of Intestacy apply

is there a living spouse?

Yes------------------------No

Any children?   Any children?

Yes----------No   Yes---------No

Spouse   Any Parents/Brothers/   Everything   Parents
Chattels   Sisters   to the
£75,000   Children
                Yes--------No

50% of   Spouse   --------Everything to
residue   Chattels   Spouse
                £125,000
                Parents 50%
                residue

There now follows a detailed explanation of what actually happens – please feel free to pass over this section unless you are interested in the technicalities. This is of no importance if you have written a Will.

RULES OF INTESTACY

ENGLAND AND WALES
If deceased dies leaving:
1. Spouse but no issue, parent, brother or sister, nephew or niece. ('issue' means children, including illegitimate and adopted children, grandchildren and so on) – but *not* step-children.

Persons who benefit:
a) Spouse takes everything absolutely.

If deceased dies leaving:
2. Spouse and issue

Persons who benefit:
a) Spouse takes personal chattels (car, furniture, pictures, clothing, jewellery etc). Plus £75,000 absolutely. Plus life interest (income only) in half of the residue (ie. balance).
b) Issue takes half residue on reaching age eighteen or marrying before age eighteen. Plus half residue on death of spouse.

If deceased dies leaving:
3. Spouse, no issue but parent(s), or brother(s), or sister(s), or nephew(s), or niece(s).
Persons who benefit:
a) Spouse takes personal chattels plus £125,000 absolutely. Plus half residue absolutely.
b) Parent(s), failing a parent then brothers and sisters (nephews and nieces step into their parents' shoes if the latter are dead) take half residue.

Note: Where part of the residuary estate includes a dwelling-house in which the surviving spouse was resident at the date of death the spouse has the right to have the dwelling-house as part of the absolute interest or towards the capital value of the life interest under 2(a) and 3(a) above.

If deceased dies leaving:
4. No Spouse.
Persons who benefit:
a) Everything is taken by Issue – but if none: Parents – but if none: Brothers and Sisters (nephews and nieces step into their parents' shoes) – but if none: Grandparents – but if none: Uncles and Aunts (cousins step into their parents' shoes) – but if none: The Crown.

LEGAL RIGHTS
These are the rights that may be claimed by a surviving

spouse and/or children, and are claimed out of the movable part of the estate (ie. property which can be moved – not land and house). The amount granted under this right is dependent upon whether the deceased is survived by only a spouse or only children or both.

* If the spouse alone survives, his or her Legal Rights will amount to one half of the remainder of the movable property after deduction of the Prior Rights of money and furniture. This is known as *'Jus Relictae'* or *'Jus Relicti'*.
* If only children survive, they will be entitled to one half of the movable estate equally between them. Children include illegitimate children and adopted children but not stepchildren. Children's Legal Rights are sometimes known as *'Legitim'* and an added complication in the calculation of 'Legitim is the procedure known as *'Collation inter Libros'*. Quite simply, this means that if the deceased parent has already given a child a substantial gift during his lifetime, its value at that time may be offset against that child's entitlement to Legal Rights.
* If both the spouse and children survive then the movable estate, less the Prior Rights so far as taken from the movable estate, is divided into equal parts. One third goes to the widow/er, one third is divided between the children and the remaining third is divided as part of the free estate.
* The 'free estate' is the heritable (ie. land and houses) and movable estate less Prior and Legal Rights.

DIVISION OF THE FREE ESTATE

The remainder of the property (the free estate) will be divided in the following manner:

Everything is taken by:

a) the children, but if none:

b) parents and brothers and sisters (half to parents, half to brothers and sisters). If there are no parents the brothers and sisters take the balance, and if there are no brothers or sisters then the parents take the balance. If there are no brothers and sisters or parents:

c) the surviving spouse, but if none:

d) uncles and aunts, but if none:

e) grandparents, but if none:

f) brothers and sisters of grandparents, but if none:
g) more remote ancestors of the intestate, but if none:
h) the Crown – if no relations can be found then the Crown takes the estate as ultimate heir.

Representation

In applying the scheme to Prior Rights, Legal Rights and division of the Free Estate it should be noted that issue are entitled by representation to take the share of the parent who has died.

Note:

Legal Rights also apply where the deceased person has left a valid Will. The Rights cannot be extinguished by the Will.

Making Your Will

It is very important that you have professional help in writing your Will. *Contact your solicitor as soon as possible.* If you do not already have a solicitor, nor know how to choose one, then please write to me for a recommendation.

CAN YOUR FAMILY AFFORD FOR YOU NOT TO HAVE A WILL?

9

WILL THE TAXMAN BE MY MAIN BENEFICIARY WHEN I DIE?

NOW YOU HAVE IT BUT WILL YOUR CHILDREN KEEP IT?

When you are dead they cannot Tax you, they Tax your children instead.

So do not attempt a DIY Will: it is risking disaster. Do not be fuzzy about your Will or more tax will be paid than should have been.

Most men assume that their wives are their beneficiaries. Most widows can tell them differently, because:

a) A wife (widow), as you have already seen, is not automatically the main beneficiary; a fact which many widows have found to their cost.

b) A Will can save a lot of time and aggravation.

c) Your estate goes where you want it.

d) A Will can reduce the amount of tax to be paid (Inheritance Tax).

So a Will is, like Life Assurance, one of the most unselfish things that you can do since it does not benefit you, it benefits your loved ones.

SOME EXAMPLES OF SIMPLE WILL PLANNING (1991/92)

A married man who owns the marital home and has two children dies intestate. His total estate value is £415,000, including £200,000 of Life Protection.

1. Without a Will being made, the rules of intestacy apply.

This means:
a) the widow receives £75,000 only, after six to twelve months and any IHT has been paid.
b) the rest is divided into two halves and taxed as follows:

i) the first half (£170,000) is held in Trust, for the children, with your widow having a right to the income whilst she lives (she can take a lump sum in lieu of the life interest).
As the income belongs to the widow for life the £170,000 cannot be touched by ANYONE until her death.
ii) of the second half the first £140,000 is taxed at 0 per cent;
iii) the next £30,000 at 40 per cent ie. £12,000.

c) the estate therefore receives, in this case, £158,000 which goes to the children ie. £79,000 each – £4000 each more than their mother receives.

Therefore the widow receives in total £75,000 plus the income from £170,000 ie. around £8500 (not indexed) for life.

SUMMARY (1991/92)
ESTATE	£415,000
WIDOW RECEIVES	£ 75,000
REMAINING ESTATE	£340,000
50% INTO TRUST – for the children	£170,000
CHILDRENS' SHARE	£170,000
TAXED AS FOLLOWS	
Nil to £140,000 at 0%	NIL
£140,000 to £170,000 at 40%	£ 12,000

Invested for the widow: £170,000 giving her an income of around £8500 for life, thus also preventing the children from using half their capital.

IF BOTH PARENTS DIE TOGETHER

ESTATE	£415,000
TAXED AS FOLLOWS	
Nil to £140,000	NIL
£140,000 to £415,000 at 40%	£110,000

This represents 26.5 per cent of the total estate going in tax.

SIMPLE USE OF A WILL

2. With a Will and Life Assurance not in Trust, the life assurance and the rest of the estate is transferred to the widow in three to six months with no problem.

SUMMARY WITH A WILL (1991/92)	
ESTATE	£415,000
WIDOW RECEIVES	£415,000
TOTAL TAXABLE	NIL
NET TRANSFER TO THE SPOUSE	£415,000

ON SECOND DEATH – OR BOTH DIE TOGETHER

3. Without a Will:
A delay of six to twelve months, and then:

SUMMARY (1991/92)	
ESTATE	£415,000
TOTAL TAXABLE	£415,000
Nil to £140,000 at 0%	NIL
£140,000 to £415,000 at 40%	£110,000
Net transfer to the estate	£305,000

4. With a Will – both dead:
The same tax position but the delay is reduced to three to six months (assuming that the estate is to be divided equally).

5. With a Trust (if there is a life policy of £200,000 in trust):
   a) the £200,000 is transferred Tax Free (£100,000 to each child) immediately;
   b) The estate is reduced by this amount for tax purposes ie. £215,000, of which £140,000 is tax free, leaving £75,000 to be taxed ie. just £30,000 in IHT a saving of £80,000.

SUMMARY WITH A TRUST (1991/92)

ESTATE	£415,000
IMMEDIATE TRUST TRANSFER	£200,000
TOTAL TAXABLE	£215,000
Nil to £140,000 at 0%	NIL
£140,000 to £215,000 at 40%	£ 30,000
Net transfer to the estate	£385,000

This simple use of a trust has:
i) given an immediate transfer of £200,000;
ii) reduced the IHT payable by £80,000 (from £110,000 to £30,000)
iii) increased the transfer by £80,000 (from £305,000 to £385,000)
iv) removed any cash flow problems.

WILLS AND THE SINGLE PERSON (ONE PARENT FAMILY)

On the death of a spouse or after a divorce, it is very important that your Will is reconsidered.

In the case of divorce, your ex-spouse has certain rights that may not be to your liking. By rewriting your Will, with professional help, it is possible to ensure that your wishes are followed.

Here I am unable to give any particular example, as this instance is fraught with difficulties. The only advice I can offer, is to say: *see a solicitor who is very experienced in writing Wills*.

WIDOWS/WIDOWERS

Any transfer to your children will be liable to IHT, so great consideration should be given to gifting, discretionary trusts and creating a fund to pay the potential liability.

GIFTING (this also applies to married couples)

By making gifts of up to the nil rate band and hoping that you live seven years, this can be very effective, but it does mean that you must no longer have the use of, nor any benefit from, the gift. Using this method of reducing the potential IHT payable may possibly result in a reduced standard of living in the future if you get your sums wrong. So great care MUST be taken before any gifts are made.

THE NIL RATE BAND DISCRETIONARY TRUST

By arranging for assets equal to the nil rate band to be placed into a discretionary trust (with your executors as trustees) for the various people you want to benefit, your executors then decide who is to inherit (from within your nominated range of beneficiaries) after your death but in accordance with your wishes. The executors then have time to make a decision on the best route for your gift.

FUNDING FOR THE INHERITANCE TAX LIABILITY

Instead of finding ways of reducing your liability, it is possible to fund for this, by the use of a suitable life policy written into an appropriate trust. If you wish a total transfer of your estate and the penalties of such planning are not to your liking, you can take out a Joint Life Second Death Life Assurance policy. It probably costs much less than you think, depending of course on age and health.

    The cost of such policies can, after the first payment, be assigned to the beneficiaries and therefore need cost you virtually nothing.

EXAMPLE 1

A male and female both aged fifty next birthday, both non-smokers, on a joint life second death basis ie. this means that it only pays out on the death of the second partner, have IHT Liability of £100,000. This can be done for a monthly premium of around £15.

The premium would have to be paid for 555 years to reach the cost of doing nothing (ie. 15 x 12 = 180; £100,000 ÷ 180 = 555.55).

EXAMPLE 2

A female aged fifty next birthday, non-smoker, has IHT Liability of £100,000 with a monthly premium of approximately £40.

The premium would have to be paid for over 200 years to reach the cost of doing nothing (ie. 40 x 12 = 480; £100,000 ÷ 480 = 208.33).

LOOKING AFTER THE CHILDREN

Most of us put off writing a Will, and almost nobody writes one in the most tax efficient manner. In a busy world it can always be demoted behind what we think are more urgent matters.

If you die without making a Will you die 'intestate', and the Inland Revenue do not distribute your estate in quite the same way as you would have. The absence of clear instructions can also lead to disputes within the family which can be emotionally draining and very expensive to resolve.

The principal object of making a Will is to ensure that your assets pass on in accordance with your wishes. The Will governs the passing on of all assets, save for assets held in trust, and some assets owned jointly with another person, which may pass automatically to the survivor of the joint owners.

Before considering how to construct a tax efficient Will, let us look briefly at the Inheritance Tax (IHT) rules. When you die, IHT is payable on the whole of your estate, including the house, savings and the proceeds of Life Policies not written into trust for named beneficiaries. If your life policies are not written into trust, doing so could be a way of saving your family a great deal of time and money.

Assets passed to your spouse are normally exempt from IHT, as are legacies to charities. This means that no tax is payable on the death of a husband who leaves his entire estate to his wife. Many people break off their planning at this point and settle for leaving everything to their spouse.

The latter may seem satisfactory but can be shortsighted. This method causes the opportunity to pass on an amount up to the Nil rate band (£140,000 – 1991/92) tax free, on the first death, to be lost. IHT will then be payable on the second death on the proportion of the estate that exceeds the then Nil rate band. In fact, this short term solution may store up problems for the children.

Anyone who reckons they are too poor to fall into the IHT net should ask himself how much his or her house is worth: you can have a modest income but, because of your house, be a sitting target for this little understood tax.

Some assets attract tax relief and so their value is reduced for IHT purposes; particularly a business, which can include an interest in a partnership or a sole trader, and agricultural land.

A Will should then be written in the context of one's overall financial and family circumstances. In particular, it should take into account the tax consequences – above all IHT. Some decisions can remove IHT altogether and others provide for its payment in a less painful way, mainly through Life Assurance.

IHT can also be whittled away by use of annual exemptions and the seven year rule.

Additional Points for Couples who wish to give their Children Maximum Protection:

1. Parents with young children should bear in mind when choosing friends, relatives or professional advisers to be executors that, on the death of the second parent, the executors will not only be responsible for the administration of the estate but will become trustees who will need to look after the financial welfare of the children.

2. The parents also need to decide on the appointment of guardians who would have custody of children under age

eighteen, in the event of the death of both parents. You may think this event is unlikely, but there is no reason to avoid making such a fundamental decision, and after all, it will cost you very little time or money.

3. A Will should also state that the husband and wife will each leave the residue of their estate to the other – assuming that is their wish. It would be recommended that the survivor only becomes entitled to the estate if they survive the other partner by thirty days. The reason for this suggestion is that it avoids the aggregation of the two estates, with the consequent Inheritance Tax disadvantages, should both parents die within a short period of each other ie. if both were involved in a car accident.

4. Their Wills should then go on to state what is to happen on the death of the survivor. In most cases the parents would probably want the residuary estate to pass to the children at a specified age, but not necessarily, in equal shares. Any age can be selected. However, whatever age is selected, the children will normally be entitled to the income from their share of the estate from the age of eighteen.

5. The Will should also include what is often termed as a 'long stop provision', in the case of an accident to the entire family. The parents will need to decide who should inherit their estates. Possibly they may decide to divide their joint assets in appropriate proportions between their two families, leaving assets to either brothers, sisters or to their parents – although the latter decision may have Inheritance Tax disadvantages.

How to cut down that tax

Let us assume that both husband and wife are aged fifty, with two children aged eighteen and twenty, neither of whom are married. The husband has a high income; the wife has none. Assets consist of the house (value £250,000) owned by the husband and wife in equal shares, and capital of £150,000, divided equally and invested in unit trusts and in building society accounts.

If the husband dies first and his entire estate passes to his wife, no IHT is payable, but on her death the IHT payable by their children would be £64,000 (1991/92).

If the husband had left, say £50,000, direct to his children, then the IHT on the death of his widow would have been reduced by £20,000 (40 per cent of £50,000). But all IHT savings have to be weighed against what you wish to happen. A Will should never be drafted purely on tax considerations, but in the most tax efficient way of doing what you want.

Consideration to be taken into account might include the ages and financial requirements of the children, and whether the wife is to continue to live in the home, or wishes to move somewhere smaller, thereby possibly releasing capital which might be surplus to requirements and could therefore be made available to the children. The ability to use a deed of variation should be taken into account.

If you decide that the wife needs all the £150,000 capital, it might be suitable for each to leave their half share of their home to the children. A value of £125,000 will then pass on the husband's death with no IHT liability. IHT should then be reduced, on the second death, by £50,000.

On the death of the husband the house would be jointly owned by the widow and the children but the widow would have the right to remain there for life.

The family would need to accept that the children would be entitled to 50 per cent of the house value, if it were sold in order for the widow to move somewhere smaller. It is also possible that the wife could have insufficient funds and the children would be under no legal obligation to share their proceeds with her. This strategy therefore carries a degree of risk as the price for saving IHT.

An alternative is for each parent to write a Will so that on the first death £75,000 passes to a discretionary trust, of which the beneficiaries will be the survivor, children, grandchildren (whether or not born) and anyone else they may wish.

Assuming the husband dies first, his executors would then become trustees of the trust; they would then invest the £75,000 and distribute the income amongst the beneficiaries as they think fit. Capital could also be paid out. In this way the widow could still be provided for. In this case, a distinct advantage is that the £75,000 will not attract an IHT liability on the husband's death, nor should it during the wife's lifeterm, nor on her death. As a result of this measure the IHT saving on her death would be £30,000.

Assuming the parents wish to leave all, or at least a large

portion of their estate to each other, in the event of the husband's death the capital will be available to the widow along with her own share for her to do as she wished.

One alternative is for the husband to leave his widow the income from his estate during her lifetime, so that the capital will then pass to the children on her death. Possibly the trustees would be given power to pay out part or all of the capital to the wife during her lifetime if she so wished. This would create a trust under the Will, of which the executors would be trustees. The trustees would then be responsible for investing the trust funds. Tax returns may also need to be submitted. A certain amount of additional expense and complication would therefore be inevitable.

Both husband and wife really need to have some assets of their own, so that, on the first death, there is scope for passing assets onto the children by means of a deed of variation (if the survivor feels that this can be afforded).

If all the assets are owned by the husband, if he were to die first then an IHT saving can be made by making use of the nil band rate, up to which £140,000 (1991/92) will be available on his death. However, if the wife dies first then she will have no assets to pass on to the children and any chance of reducing the potential liability will be lost. The placing of assets up the value of the Nil rate band into an 'Executor's discretionary trust' should always be considered.

The ownership of assets, and your Will, should constantly be reviewed.

WOULD YOU LIKE TO DIS-INHERIT THE TAXMAN?

YES!

THEN SEE YOUR SOLICITOR TODAY

10

SIMPLE USE OF FLEXIBLE TRUSTS

HOW WOULD YOU LIKE YOUR FAMILY TO REMEMBER YOU?

QUESTION:
How can I ensure that the benefits from this life policy end up tax free in the hands of whomsoever I wish?

ANSWER:
Often by the use of the appropriate Trust.

WHAT IS A TRUST?
A Trust is a method of transferring assets from one person to another quickly and in a very tax efficient manner.

They are often used with agricultural and business properties to ensure that the full value of the assets are transferred, and also in Inheritance Tax and life assurance planning.

WHEN SHOULD A TRUST BE USED?
This question is really too great to be answered within the scope of this book. All that I am willing to say, is that you contact a good professional Financial Adviser to give you specific help and advice.

What I shall do is give two simple examples which I hope will convince you to consider making use of a Trust.

WHAT CAN A TRUST DO?
It can take assets out of the estate before the Will is proved, that is, before probate, for Inheritance Tax purposes.

EFFECT OF USING A TRUST
The assets are transferred immediately (no waiting for probate) and often completely tax free.

SIMPLE USE OF A FLEXIBLE TRUST
Great care must be taken, and expert advice must always be sought. It is not as simple as it appears.

EXAMPLES (1991/92)

1. ASSUMPTIONS – Husband and wife die together

	(i) NO TRUST	(ii) TRUST
Estate value	£140,000	£140,000
Life Assurance	£100,000	£100,000
Gross Estate	£240,000	£240,000
Taxable Estate	£240,000	£140,000
Tax payable		
Nil to £140,000 at 0%	NIL	NIL
£140,000 to £240,000 at 40%	£ 40,000	NIL
Therefore total transfer	£200,000	£240,000

(i) No Trust Route
No monies would be transferred to the estate until the IHT had been paid; depending on whether there was a Will or not probate would take six to nine months.

Inheritance tax of £40,000 is payable, equivalent to 16.66 per cent of the gross estate.

(ii) Trust Route
If the life assurance had been placed into a flexible trust at no cost to the client, the Inland Revenue would not regard the £100,000 as part of the client's estate as far as Inheritance Tax is concerned. Therefore the whole of the £100,000 would be transferred intact (tax free) to the client's beneficiaries without any probate delay.

If the husband alone had died, leaving everything to his wife in his Will, his widow would have had no tax disadvantages ie. no IHT on transfers between husband and wife, but she would have received the £100,000 immediately without waiting for probate.

If the client had left no Will, then there would be delays connected with the £140,000 estate.

2. This next situation is a development of an earlier example.

A married couple with three children die. Their total estate value is £415,000 including £200,000 life assurance.

	(i) NO TRUST	(ii) IN TRUST
Estate	£215,000	£215,000
Life Assurance	£200,000	£200,000
Taxable estate	£415,000	£215,000
Inheritance Tax payable*	£110,000	£ 30,000

Effect of the Trust
  a) Reduction in Tax payable of £80,000
  b) Immediate tax free transfer, to the children, of £200,000 without any probate delay.

* *Simplified calculations:*
£415,000 - £140,000 = £275,000 x 40% = £110,000
£215,000 - £140,000 = £ 75,000 x 40% = £ 30,000

WHEN SHOULD I PLACE A LIFE POLICY INTO TRUST?

In every case it is sensible to consider placing a life policy in a suitably designed trust, except where the policy is to be used immediately, or in the near future as collateral security eg. to support a bank loan or a mortgage advance.

Again you will need Professional Advice before any decision is made.

WHAT HAPPENS IF I CHANGE MY MIND?

In most cases this causes a problem. Whilst Trusts are easy to set up, they are difficult or even impossible to dismantle, so great care has to be taken to get it right in the first place.

The following explains the technicalities - again please free to pass over this section if you are not interested in the actualities.

FLEXIBLE TRUSTS AND TAX PLANNING

WHEN DOES A TRUST EXIST?

A trust exists where the owner of property (the 'settlor') arranges for one or more trustees to hold that property (eg. a life policy) on behalf of one or more beneficiaries.

The settlor (or settlors) may be the trustee(s) but, having declared a trust over the trust property, the settlor ceases to be its absolute owner. The trustees enjoy the legal ownership, but it is a restricted right since the trust property is held entirely on behalf of the beneficiary or beneficiaries, and can only be dealt with in accordance with the trust provisions.

Example:

Mr Smith takes out a life policy for £100,000. He writes it in trust for the benefit of his two children, the trustees being himself, his wife and his solicitor.

The policy no longer belongs to Mr Smith, even though he pays the premiums. It is owned by the three trustees jointly, but the trustees have to hold it (or its proceeds) for the benefit of Mr Smith's two children.

WHY PLACE A POLICY IN TRUST?

There are seven main reasons:

(i) to give away the value represented by the policy (its surrender value or its sum assured) whilst giving the trustees some control over the policy and its proceeds, thereby ensuring that they are neither misused nor wasted by the beneficiary or beneficiaries.

(ii) To afford the trust property some degree of protection from the settler's creditors.

(iii) To reduce the delay when settling a claim on the settlor's death, so that the life office pays the surviving trustee(s) on proof of the settlor's death, without waiting for the personal representative(s) to obtain the appropriate Court Order eg. a grant of probate.

(iv) To reduce the Inheritance Tax on the settlor's death by ensuring that the proceeds of the life policy form no part of the settlor's personal estate. In this case, to be effective, the trust must not have any reversion or rights or possible benefits to the settlor. The policy proceeds can then pass free of inheritance tax to the trust beneficiary or beneficiaries.

Example:
In the previous example the life office will pay out the sum assured on Mr Smith's death. Payment will be to the trustee(s) who will then hold the proceeds on behalf of the beneficiaries, ie. Mr Smith's two children. At no time will the proceeds be treated as part of Mr Smith's assets and, therefore, there will be no Inheritance Tax payable on the proceeds as a result of Mr Smith's death.

Had the policy not been written in trust, the sum assured would have been payable to Mr Smith's personal representatives, and the money would therefore have formed part of his assets when calculating the liability to IHT triggered by his death. During 1990/91 the highest rate of tax was 40 per cent, and so by writing the policy in trust a saving of up to £40,000 would have been achieved.

(v) To maximize the opportunities for IHT mitigation by way of lifetime gifts using the available allowances and exemptions (eg. the annual allowance and the normal expenditure out of income exemption) to cover premiums where possible.

Example:
In Mr Smith's case, his payment of premiums on the trust policy will be treated as gifts to the trust, since the trust benefits from the payment to the life office and he does not. However, the payments can probably be absorbed within his annual allowance or the normal expenditure out of income exemption.

Had the policy not been in trust the premiums would not have been treated as gifts, Mr Smith being both the payer and the beneficiary. Consequently, the premiums could not have used part or all of the annual allowance and they would have effectively remained in Mr Smith's estate.

(vi) To facilitate the provision of business assurance eg. the use of suitable trusts is often necessary in providing Keyman cover, Shareholder assurance and Partnership assurance.

(vii) To provide liquid cash to pay all debts including

Inheritance Tax without needing to arrange probate loans and pay interest.

Note:

If the settlor is using ordinary life policies under trust as part of an IHT planning exercise it is essential that he or she is entirely excluded from benefit. Where a benefit is retained the trust may not be effective, for IHT purposes, in taking the trust property out of the settlor's estate.

WHAT IS THE MAIN FEATURE OF A FLEXIBLE TRUST?

The flexible trust enables the settlor to place a life policy in trust for the beneficiaries referred to in section A and B. However, it also permits the trustees to change the beneficiaries within the nominated range. Consequently, the beneficiary's(ies') interests are not fixed and can be varied to suit changing circumstances.

Although at first glance the flexible trust may look like a discretionary trust, its tax treatment is different and therefore not subject to a potentially onerous tax treatment (ten year charge).

SAVE TIME SAVE TAX: USE A TRUST

BUT DO SEE A PROFESSIONAL ADVISER FIRST!

11

HOW DO I ARRANGE MY AFFAIRS FOR BOTH LIFE AND DEATH?

IF I DO NOT KNOW WHAT I HAVE HOW DO I KNOW WHAT I CAN DO WITH IT?

MY PERSONAL BUSINESS PLAN REVIEW BOOKLET

One of the most neglected areas in financial planning is the lack of an effective recording and planning system. A simple accurate easily used method is essential in order to keep you informed as to where you are, whether or not you are on target and where you want to be.

I have developed such a system, called Private Client Portfolio, that not only helps you to steer your financial course but also acts as an invaluable guide to your executors, trustees, guardians and professional advisers (this system is available to other professional advisers both in hard copy and disc form under a licence agreement).

The system has been described, by members of the Law Society, as, 'the perfect estate organizer especially for unqualified executors' and by members of the Insurance industry as, 'the Bible for our Industry'.

An example of how effective this type of planning is can be found in Chapter Four. John (not his real name) came to me about two years after a friend had recommended him to. The delay was caused by the fact that he was happy with his existing adviser and nothing could be done for him, needless to say he changed his mind. There was nothing actually wrong with his portfolio. It was the way that it was done – in the

words of the song:
'It ain't what you do it's the way that you do it'.

Space prevents the reproduction of a full booklet but please do study the next few pages very closely:

INDEX
Needs no explanation.

IN THE EVENT OF MY DEATH
List here your Executors, Trustees, Guardians and anyone else that would be required in the event of your death together with their addresses telephone numbers.

PROFESSIONAL ADVISERS
List all your professional advisers together with addresses and telephone numbers.

BANKS AND BUILDING SOCIETIES
Here you must record full information on all the accounts you hold, whether or not they are joint and what signatories there are. There is no need to record balances.

CLUBS AND SOCIETIES
The reason for this is to prevent your beneficiaries being contacted causing upset and to stop any fees that are no longer due because of your death. Many times I have found that widows are still paying by direct debit fees for a club that their husband used to be a member of before he died.

FAMILY DETAILS
Basically who is in your Will again with addresses and telephone numbers.

BUSINESS DETAILS
The names of people to contact at work eg. Personnel Officer. Other details such as NI number, tax reference number and tax office address.

IMPORTANT INFORMATION
Where all your important documents are kept together with any other personal information you wish.

PERSONAL BUDGET

Full details of current income and expenditure together with what the position would be if only the husband was alive and if only the wife was alive. There is surprisingly little difference between the three positions as the saying goes 'Two can live as cheaply as one'; it can also be said 'That one can live as expensively as two'.

BALANCE SHEET

A list of all assets and liabilities showing your net worth.

REGULAR OUTGOINGS

A list of all your regular outgoings, their frequency, purpose, start and end date.

INDEPENDENT TAXATION

A summary of your position and a study of the possibility of transferring assets from one spouse to the other.
Your adviser will be needed for this section.

FINANCIAL REQUIREMENTS

What you would like to happen financially in the event of your long term illness, in retirement and in the event of your death.
Your adviser will be needed for this section.

CURRENT SITUATION

What would happen now in the event of your illness or death. Your anticipated position on reaching retirement.
Your adviser will be needed for this section.

OVERALL SITUATION

A comparison of the previous two showing the problem if any.
Your adviser will be needed for this section.

FINANCIAL PLAN

What to do to rectify the problem.
Your adviser will be needed for this section.

ESTATE VALUATION

A summary of your Inheritance Tax position before you planned and one for after your planning is done.

Your adviser will be needed for this section.

SUMMARY

A very detailed resume of the position if you are ill, if you die, when your mortgage is finished and in retirement. Figures here must be in cash and value terms.

Your adviser will be needed for this section.

POLICY LIST

A complete list of all your insurance policies and investments together with start and anticipated maturity dates.

Your adviser will be needed for this section.

MORTGAGE

Full information on your mortgage loan, the lender, interest rate, penalties and other options.

Your adviser will be needed for this section.

ENDOWMENT

Full details of any repayment method (I have chosen to call it Endowment because this is now the most popular route although I seldom recommend it myself because there are more IHT effective ways). Also, very importantly the reason for the policy.

I enclose a sample page here to show in more detail what I mean.

Your adviser will be needed for this section.

Next follows a similar page for every single policy that you have be it life, pension or general insurance.

PERSONAL PENSION

Your adviser will again be needed to collect the information from the relevant insurance companies and then assess it for you. This page should give you reason for the plan as well as its value and will need updating at least once a year.

Beneficiary
Life Assured
Policy Ownership
Date of Birth
Age Admitted
Insurance Company
Policy Number
Sum Assured
Investment
Fund Link
Start Date
Maturity Date
Single Investment
Regular Investment
Increasing   %
Contribution Protected   months
Frequency
How Payable
Current Value
Maturity Value
Pension of
Or   A Tax Free Lump Sum
Plus A Pension of
Pension in Trust
Life Cover in Trust
Life Cover Assigned
Purpose of the Pension and Life Cover

FINANCIAL PLANNING IS ONLY ORGANIZED COMMON SENSE

12

WHAT SHOULD I EXPECT FROM MY FINANCIAL ADVISER?

> *'Your adviser owes you, not his industry only, but his judgment, and he betrays instead of serving you, if he sacrifices it to your opinion'*
> Edmund Burke

Never go along with an adviser who agrees with everything you say. He could be as unskilled as you. To show the problem with this sort of adviser I will repeat my statistics from the first review of clients' portfolios:

* 91 per cent needed some form of amendment.
* 87 per cent needed to be age admitted.
* 75 per cent of Life Protection policies should have been placed into Trust at outset – 87 per cent of these were placed into Trust on my first review.
* 90 per cent of Personal Pension funds should have been placed into trust at outset – 99 per cent of these were placed into Trust on my first review.
* 13 per cent of Savings type life policies should have been placed into Trust at outset – few were placed into Trust because of changes in legislation.
* 68 per cent of Executive type pensions were not set up correctly – because of lack of communication between the Company's solicitor and its pension adviser: this will be explained fully in the business version to follow.
* 81 per cent of Partnerships had no protection for the partners.

* 69 per cent of Private Limited Companies had no protection for their Directors or Shares.
* 76 per cent of Firms had no protection for their Key-men.
* 76 per cent of Clients had no Will – 19 per cent of those with a Will needed it to be modified or re-written.
* No mortgages were planned with Inheritance Tax in mind.

These figures tend to confirm my previous statement that too many policies are bought for the wrong reasons and from the wrong people. Although the Financial Services Act of 1986 had good intentions, it has fallen far short of what is needed. Our financial industry certainly needs to be put into better order, although established 'respectable' professions, such as solicitors, stockbrokers, financiers and bankers, actually seem to have as many problems.

The best I can do is to help you make a decision on how good your current Financial Adviser is and how competent he or she is. If you do not already have a Professional Adviser I can help you to choose one.

HOW MUCH DOES A FINANCIAL ADVISER COST?

Most good financial advisers make no charge for the first meeting, since it is intended purely to ascertain whether or not their services are needed, and if so, the method and amount of payment agreed. Never be afraid of approaching a financial adviser on the grounds of cost.

As to the actual cost, most professionals like myself work by fees. These fees are offset by payments from the companies with whom business is placed. This often results in the client having to make no actual payment to us. Any surplus commissions are rebated into the policy.

A system such as this, as opposed to commission or fees only, seems to suit the majority of clients, as it involves them in the minimum initial costs, in addition to removing any fear of having to find a large sum of money.

Your circumstances continually change, so advice is needed on a regular basis. I usually suggest that my clients complete a standing monthly order to cover the cost of all future visits, to ensure that tax affairs are kept up to date, and that their Will is reviewed annually and rewritten where necessary, together with another full financial review completed.

If any further business is transacted, it will be on normal business terms, as already discussed with the client. There is no actual requirement for my clients to pay the monthly charge if they do not require the additional services.

SOME FINANCIAL ADVISERS CAN CAUSE MORE PROBLEMS THAN THEY SOLVE

I will quote an example of this:

One evening on my way home from the office I called into a pub for a drink. While I was there I started talking to a man who asked me what I did, when he was told he laughed saying, 'You are too late, you cannot sell me anything because I have just taken out a policy for £150,000 to protect my children now that I am divorced.'

When asked if the policy was in Trust he said no, when it was pointed out that, in his case over £49,000 (1988/89) would go in tax, after about six months delay, however if he made use of the correct trust he could not only save £49,000 tax he would also ensure an immediate transfer.

After we placed his policy into Trust (at no charge), guess whose client he and his five partners are now?

1. You may be sold unsuitable products

As no formal training is required nor any qualifications needed, many 'financial advisers' are not, to put it politely, good enough, because they have not had the training necessary.

2. They act outside their area of expertize

Many still proceed to advise and make recommendations, even when they realize (or worse still, do not realize) that they have insufficient knowledge. There could be several reasons for this:

a) they do not wish to share the commission;
b) they are frightened of losing the business.

3. Failure to age admit

If the insurance company has not seen your birth/marriage certificates, they will not pay out the proceeds of the policy either on death or on maturity. It is therefore essential that ALL policies are age admitted at the outset or as soon as possible thereafter. You may have noticed that all lenders insist that all policies to be assigned to them are age admitted: they know the problem and delays caused by not doing so.

4. Failure to service the client at least once a year

Circumstances change continually, so regular contact is needed to keep the client up-to-date and well-informed, and to explain again just what the financial adviser has done and why.

5. Insufficient attention to the tax effects of the plan on either death or maturity

Different plans have totally different tax treatment either on maturity, partial surrender, early surrender or on death. Each has to be considered and explained.

6. Lack of use of Trusts

Trusts are one of the most efficient ways of transferring assets from one person to another, both from the time and tax points of view. They should be considered when every life policy is taken out. If a decision is made not to put the policy into trust, then this should be reconsidered at least once a year. If the policy is placed into a flexible trust then the trustees should be reviewed annually or in the event of the death of any of them. It might be appropriate to write a letter stating your wishes on an annual basis, to give the trustees guidance as to your current plans.

7. Little knowledge of the rules in intestacy

It is surprising that a large number of financial advisers have no idea of the rules of intestacy. This being the case, how can they profess to be financial advisers? They sell you £150,000 of life assurance but neglect to tell you that if both husband and wife die, assuming the rest of your estate is worth at least £140,000 (1991/92), 40 per cent ie. £60,000 will disappear in tax after a wait of up to six to nine months. In most cases, they neglect to tell you of this because they do not realize themselves. Yet the use of the correct trust (not always an easy choice) can ensure that all £150,000 would be transferred to whomsoever you wish, both tax free and immediately (no probate delays).

8. Insufficient use of Wills in financial planning

Your Will is probably the most important aspect of your financial planning, since, as I have already stated, the government, and not you, will decide what happens to your estate should you die intestate. Having said that, financial advisers seldom stress just how important it is for you to make your Will. You have already seen how, under the rules of intestacy, your widow is not necessarily your main beneficiary.

I must mention here that several companies have set up 'cold call selling', for Wills to be delivered, in many cases, by life assurance salesmen: this is an easy way for the salesman to sell life policies to the client and also to any witnesses. Such Wills are computer generated ie. the salesman is not the person who actually draws up the Will. This split responsibility and complete reliance on computer programs is a potential area for problems for you, no matter how good the basic system. However, even most of these Wills would be much better than the application of the rules of intestacy.

YOUR WILL IS VERY IMPORTANT: IT MUST BE WRITTEN PROPERLY BY A PROFESSIONAL. Choose a solicitor who specializes in writing Wills – not all solicitors handle enough to be fully competent.

I can assure you that the cost of not writing a Will is far

higher, both financially and emotionally, than the cost of writing a Will. Why leave an unnecessary problem for your family?

9. Little or no co-operation with other professionals

Because our industry is, unfortunately, mainly sales orientated, many financial advisers shy away from co-operation with other professionals and are worried, in many cases correctly, that other professionals will take the business.

Accountants have often told me that they have great difficulty in keeping up to date in their own subject (and in fact, that is why so many of them decide to specialize), yet at the same time they attempt to give advice in our field. Several solicitors have also stated that professional companies, such as estate agents and building societies, should not practise conveyancing but stick to their own areas of expertize – yet there are solicitors who see themselves as experts in financial advice.

It is impossible for any one person to be fully competent in more than one area of expertize.

It is important that these professionals realize exactly what they don't know, and refer clients to fellow professionals with specialist knowledge of those fields.

Ted Spratt's Guide to Financial Planning uses the above principle. It uses the expertize of all the professional services by co-operation with them as opposed to confrontation and mistrust.

10. Failure to keep up to date with the latest legislation

There are so many changes in our industry that it is almost a full time job keeping up to date. Your adviser is more likely to be cognisant of those changes if he wishes to co-operate with your other advisers than if he wishes to avoid them.

11. Tend to do what the client asks for rather than what is best for the client

Having said that, what you want sometimes takes

precedence over what you need, but your adviser is duty bound to show you.

Whilst not complete, the above points give you an idea of the main problem areas.

QUESTIONS TO ASK YOUR FINANCIAL ADVISER

Is he or she independent* or is he or she tied**?

If he or she is tied, to whom?

A. You and Your Mortgage

1. Describe fully the various methods of buying a home

2. List the advantages and disadvantages of each route

3. Ask for a comparison of pension, repayment, unit trust, endowment, investment, PEP and pension routes, and explain each route fully so that I know which is the best for me and why

4. Can the premiums of my policy be increased or reduced without penalty?

5. Can the term be extended or shortened without penalty?

6. Do I have to pay the premium if I am off work ill?

7. Is it better for me (if married) to have a joint life or a single life policy and a single life term? If so, why? If not, why not?

8. Will up to 75 per cent of my salary be paid if I am ill?

---

* an independent actually and legally works for you
** a tied adviser works for an insurance company

9. Can I have a premium holiday if cash is short?

10. Will you age admit my policy/ies?

11. If two single life policies are recommended, should the term insurance be placed in Trust? If so, why? If not, why not?

12. What is the total cost of each route over the mortgage term?

13. What is the total projected return of each route?

14. What happens if I am made redundant, become ill or die?

15. Are the interest payments made for me if I am off work ill?

16. Can I take surplus equity from my policy?

17. Does the plan guarantee to pay off the mortgage?

18. Have you looked at the IHT implications? What are they?

B. You and Your Personal Pension

1. Do I need a pension? If so, why?

2. Does my spouse need a pension? If so, why?

3. Is the recommended company consistently in the top quartile?

4. Can the investment be started/stopped/ reduced/ increased at any time without penalty?

5. Will you age admit my policy?

6. What happens to my investment in the event of my death

before retirement? A return of the full fund value, and not just premiums or premiums plus 5 per cent, is generally recommended.

7. Should my fund be placed into Trust? If so, why? If not, why not?

8. Should any life assurance I take out in connection with my pension be placed into Trust? If so, why? If not, why not?

9. Can I place my pension fund into trust and leave my life assurance out of trust, as I require it as security for a mortgage?

10. Will you write my pension to the most suitable age for me?

11. Into how many sections can I divide my pension? (this gives increased flexibility on reaching retirement).

12. Can I index my contributions?

13. Is there an open market option?

14. Can I index my life protection?

15. Are my contributions paid for if I am ill, and if so, is it on an increasing basis?

16. Can I keep my life assurance after I retire?

17. How often should I review my contribution (less than 10 per cent of people review their pension annually?

You and Your Company Pension

1. What are my anticipated benefits under my scheme given my number of years service possible?

2. Can those benefits be increased?

3. What salary is my pension based on?

4. Can I pension overtime, bonuses and perks?

5. What is my death in service benefit?

6. Can it be increased? If so, how?

7. If I need to make additional contributions do they have to be through my company AVC?

8. If so, which route is the best for me and why?

9. What happens to my benefit if I change companies?

You and Monthly Savings Policies

1. Do I need a regular savings plan? If so, why?

2. Does my spouse need a regular savings plan? If so, why?

3. Which is the best type, or types, of saving vehicle for me: bank/building society/post office/unit trust/unit linked with profits/PEPs/pension? Why?

4. What is the difference in tax treatment?

5. What effect will this investment have on age allowance?

6. If a life policy is chosen, will you age admit?

7. Are the savings more beneficial in joint or in single names?

8. How will separate taxation affect our circumstances?

9. Is it beneficial to make use of a Trust? If so, why? If not, why not?

10. What is the tax treatment of the proceeds?

11. Is there any life protection?

12. Are there any penalties for not maintaining payments?

13. Is the value of the saving accessible without penalty? If not, what are the penalties?

14. Is this investment short, medium or long term?

You and Lump Sum Investments

1. Which is the best type of investment for me: bank/building society/post office/unit trust/unit linked with non-profits/PEPs/pension? Why?

2. What is the difference in tax treatment?

3. What effect will the income from this investment have on age allowance?

4. If a life policy is chosen, will you age admit?

5. Is the investment more beneficial in joint, or in single names?

6. How will separate taxation affect my circumstances?

7. Is it beneficial to make use of a Trust? If so, why? If not, why not?

8. Would it be more beneficial for an income or growth type of investment?

9. Are there any penalties on withdrawing my investment? If so, what?

10. Is it short, medium or long term investment?

11. How much risk, if any, is there with this investment?

12. Can I take an income from my investment?

13. If so, how often, and how much?

You and Life Protection

1. Do I need any Life Protection? If so, why?
2. What type and level of protection do I need for my family? Why do I need this level? Why do I need this type?
3. Will you age admit?
4. Should it be in Trust? If so, why? If not, why not?
5. What is the difference between term, convertible term and whole of life?
6. Is there a cash value? If so, what is it after ten years? And at age sixty?
7. Is there premium protection?
8. Is there indexation (premium and sums assured)?
9. Is there critical illness benefit?
10. Do I need any life protection for my business (Keyman, Loan, Partner or Share protection)?
11. If so, what type and level of protection do I need?
12. Should it be in Trust? If so, why? If not, why not?

You and Disability Protection

1. What is disability protection?
2. Do I need it? If so, why?
3. What level of protection can I have?
4. What is the tax treatment of the income?

5. Is the level of protection indexed from the start of the plan?

6. Do I have the right to increase my protection if my circumstances change without further medical evidence?

7. Will you age admit my policy?

8. To what age is the benefit written?

9. Can I have a Tax Free Lump Sum on the diagnosis of a Critical Illness?

10. What is a Critical Illness?

11. How much will I need?

12. Should I use a Trust? If so, why? If not, why not?

You and Inheritance Tax

1. Will you value my estate?

2. Will you arrange for me to have advice in connection with my Will?

3. After my Will has been written, please arrange my Will in the most tax efficient way, taking into account my wishes.

4. Is there still any liability to IHT? If so, how much?

5. Is gifting suitable for my requirements?

6. Can I take advantage of any form of Trust?

7. Should I divide our estate?

8. If there is still a liability to IHT, how can I make arrangements for it to be paid in instalments?

Financial Planning

1. Please prepare a simple review, showing exactly where and why all your recommendations fit into my overall strategy.

2. Please prepare a 'mini' review to accompany each policy, so I know exactly why I have it.

3. Please prepare an intestacy booklet.

>   WOULD YOU PREFER YOUR ADVISER
>   TO ADVISE
>   OR TO TAKE INSTRUCTIONS?

13

EXECUTOR'S GUIDE

WHAT DO I DO WHEN SOMEONE DIES?

'A man's dying is more the survivor's affair than his own.'

Thomas Mann

Death has to be certified by a doctor, who will issue a medical certificate stating the cause of death.

If a death occurs in a hospital the hospital authorities will issue a 'cause if death' certificate to the local Registration Office.

When death occurs in unusual circumstances the police should be informed but if the coroner is satisfied with the diagnosis a death certificate will be issued. On the occasions he is not satisfied a post mortem will be necessary. The post mortem needs to be completed before a death certificate can be issued.

REGISTRATION

In England and Wales the law requires that a death must be registered within five days at the local registrar's office (the address and telephone number can be found under 'Registrar of Births, Deaths and Marriages' in the local telephone book). This registration can be done by a relative of the deceased, or by an executor.

You should take to the registrar:

the death certificate, the deceased's Birth Certificate and/or National Insurance number, the Marriage Certificate (if appropriate) and details of the last occupation.

A 'Certificate of Registration' will then be issued, at no cost.

This certificate is then used to claim National Insurance benefits together with the form BD 8.

Certified copies of the entry in the register (Death Certificate) are required when applying for a 'Grant of Probate' and for Life Assurance claims. It is recommended that you buy several copies, to speed up the process of claiming monies owed to the deceased's estate (as normal photocopies are not acceptable). If further copies are required afterwards they are roughly double the cost.

When death has been registered a certificate is issued allowing a funeral to be arranged.

If no specific instructions have been left by the deceased then the decision of the type of funeral ie. cremation or burial and where, is left to the executor or the deceased's next of kin.

Members of the National Association of Funeral Directors have a code of practice which gives details of services and the costs. The minimum requirements are usually:

A coffin, a hearse, a car for mourners, bearers (to carry the coffin).

Other services can be provided at extra cost ie. Chapel of Rest.

The basic charge is from around £350.

Costs of cremation or burial must be added. Burial is the more expensive because of the plot of land or the reopening of a family grave.

With cremation you will need to pay the fees of the two doctors needed to sign the cremation certificate. And, of course, the vicar's charges.

The total cost of a basic funeral is from around £600. If a tombstone is required the costs of this must be added to the charge above.

The costs of the funeral take precedence over all other debts and can be recovered from the deceaseds estate.

Sometimes financial help with funeral costs is available.

The estate is frozen until Grant of Probate is obtained for the estate of the deceased (this is where the use of a suitable trust can be of great assistance). Grant of probate can take months or even years and as all other assets may be frozen liquid cash can be non existent.

'Financial Help', potentially taxable, is available from the

State in the form of a Widow's allowance.

A widow usually inherits her husband's basic State pension (if he was in receipt of it at the time of his death) plus any earnings related benefit.

This highlights the need for a Will and the provision of a continuing income after death (Life Assurance).

The message is clear: if you do not look after your family, no one else will.

For a 'common law wife' there is only the one parent family benefits.

For more detailed help see the end of this report.

Again it must be emphasized the importance of a valid Will correctly drawn by a solicitor. Often home made Wills, no matter how well intentioned cause problems and family disputes.

If no Will can be traced, the executors may have to advertise in the Law Society Gazette for anyone with an interest to come forward.

PROBATE

On death, all personal wealth (worldwide) apart from jointly owned assets is frozen and the personal representatives more commonly known as the executors if nominated in the Will, or if no Will then they are officially called administrators follow certain rules before the estate can pass to the heirs. Forms have to be completed for the probate office on the deceased's financial affairs, any liability to Inheritance Tax will have to be paid, a grant of probate or if no Will grant of letters of administration. This is the legal authority to arrange the deceased's estate.

As I am confident that anyone reading this book will have, by now, executed a Will, I will deal only with the procedures if a Will is in existence. But if help is needed if someone you know dies without a Will please see the end of this review.

GRANT OF PROBATE

No grant of probate is required where the estate consists of personal effects and less than £5000 in savings or where property is in joint names and can be seen to become the property of the survivor.

It is possible for you to make a personal application for probate. But is often better for the deceased's solicitor to apply especially where there are extensive interests ie. business property, agricultural property, trusts, or if the affairs are especially complex. Or if the estate is insolvent or comes to more than the Nil rate band for Inheritance Tax purposes.

At such a time, if the deceased had a review as recommended by this book much time, effort and cost can be avoided just at a time when it is appreciated most.

A Will can be contested by five groups of people:

The spouse, a common law wife, any close relations, business associates or anyone who is financially dependent.

A Will is automatically revoked on marriage unless it is clearly stated in the Will.

On divorce not all the clauses are revoked so it is especially important that the situation is reviewed. The ex-spouse is no longer an executor nor will any gift to him or her be valid.

APPLICATION FOR A GRANT OF PROBATE

An application for a grant of probate is not as bad as it first appears. Most members of the probate office are usually both helpful and understanding. The following points should help to clarify what needs to be done.

1. Open an executor's account (usually this has to be a loan account and special rates of interest can be negotiated) with the deceased's bank: this is to defer any funeral expenses, probate costs and Inheritance Tax payments.

After probate has been granted this account is used to discharge any liabilities and to receive any monies due (eg. life insurance).

It is usual for the bank and several building societies to allow the executors and deceased's accounts to be treated as one so that credit in one offsets any debit in the other. The interest charged usually qualifies for tax relief.

2. Obtain all the necessary probate forms from your local office (address will be found in the local telephone directory under registration of Births, Deaths and Marriages). The following forms are needed:
Form PR48A How to make a Personal Application for Grant of Probate
Form PR4B Probate fees payable
Form PR83 Or Form PA 1 The Grant of Probate application form.
Form Cap 44 The estate return for Inheritance Tax
Form Cap 40 Capital Taxes Office – Schedule of Stocks and Shares
Form Cap 37 Capital Taxes Office – Schedule of Real and Immovable Property.
Request booklet PA2 – How to obtain Probate

3. Value the assets.
(a) Financial statements (bank etc) showing the balances at the date of death should be obtained. Where joint accounts are held it is assumed that half the balance belonged to the deceased unless otherwise designated (this can be useful in tax planning especially with separate taxation).
(b) Life assurance companies must be informed of the date of death and a request of the value of the policies on that day and whether any are in trust. (Again if a review had been completed most of this information would be at hand. Eventually the insurance company will need a certified original of the death certificate and certified copies of any birth and marriage certificates. The last two should already have been done).
Providing the trustees are available any policies that are in trust may be encashed immediately, without waiting for probate. The value of any policy taken out by the deceased on a life of another basis also will be needed.
(c) Stocks and Shares: the value must be the closing price on the day before death and may be obtained from the financial press or London Share Services pages in the issue for the date of death. For Unit Trusts a valuation should be requested from

the fund managers. The valuation of family company shares is more difficult and help from the deceased's accountant is needed.

(d) The balance of any monies due from employment also have to be taken into account together with any pension benefits. If, however, the deceased was not drawing his personal or company pension and the fund is in trust the monies may be paid direct to the dependents of the deceased.

(e) A valuation for the home should be obtained from a local qualified surveyor and it ought to be a forced sale value on the date of death. Any outstanding mortgage should be separately stated and not deducted from the value.

(f) House contents and personal effects, all personal items (car, clothes etc) should be present at second hand value if sold, although any item on credit, eg on hire purchase, is included at its value with the instalments treated as a debt on the estate. Some valuable items will need a professional valuation.

4. Debts, funeral expenses (but not tombstones), all household bills and outstanding debts eg. overdraft, credit cards, unpaid tax and mortgage.

A recommended protective measure is to advertise in the London Gazette or a local newspaper for any creditors to submit a claim by a specific date otherwise an unpaid creditor may make a claim on the executors or beneficiaries.

5. All gifts and transfers to individuals or settlements in the seven years (Inheritance Tax legislation) to the date of death have to be declared (for IHT purposes). Certain gifts are excluded.

6. Complete Form PR83 (PA1) and Form Cap 44 and return to the Probate Personal Application Department together with the original Will and Death Certificate.

In most cases an appointment to swear the papers (the executors sign an oath that the information is to the best of their knowledge correct) is made within five weeks.

Care must be taken to read the forms through before completing as joint assets have a separate section and must not be halved in the first.

If there is no IHT the grant will soon follow.

On estates greater that £140,000 (1991/92) where IHT is payable the probate office sends the account to the Capital Taxes Office (Minford House, Rockley Road, London W14 0DF) for assessment. When the assessment is received back by the probate office an appointment to swear the papers and to pay the tax is made. The grant cannot be made until all liability to IHT has been made.

Copies, not photocopies, of the grant of probate can be obtained (for a small charge) to avoid delay in completing the administration of the estate.

Probate court fees come as an unpleasant surprise to most executors. There is the court fee for estates in excess of £25,000 and an additional charge where grant if through the Personal Application department.

PROBLEM

A grant of probate cannot be obtained until IHT is paid.

Banks, Building Societies and Insurance companies cannot release monies until grant of probate has been obtained. This is where the loan account comes into its own (unless provisions under trust have been made).

In certain cases – mainly agricultural or business – the IHT can be paid over ten years interest free.

Form 30 is the clearance certificate (issued by the Capital Taxes office) when all liability for IHT has been paid. This can be up to ten years if this option has been taken.

The Grant of Probate is signed by an officer of the Probate Registry and states:

> 'The last will and testament of the said deceased was proved and registered in the principal Probate Registry Office of the High Court of Justice and the administration of all the estate which by law devolves to and vests in the personal representative of the said deceased was granted by the aforesaid court to . . .'

A sealed (certified) copy of the Will is attached, the original is kept at Somerset House. Any member of the public can obtain a copy for a small fee.

NOW THE WORK STARTS

On production of the grant of Probate, debtors ie. Building Societies and Life Assurance companies will pay money to the estate (this is when several sealed copies of the grant can save both time and money). Bills can now be settled but executors cannot be paid for their time, unless the Will specifically allows it. However, any expenses – which includes professional advice – can be reclaimed.

It may be necessary to sell some Stocks and Shares to release cash to pay creditors – if so the services of a stockbroker are required.

If it is just a matter of transfer of ownership then the share certificates plus a sealed copy of probate together with stock transfer forms duly stamped should be sent to the company concerned. A new certificate will then be issued.

The same process applies to Gilt-Edged Securities but in this case the information is sent to the Bank of England.

Having paid all debts the executor is then free to distribute the remainder in accordance with the instructions in the Will.

If there is a minor (person under age eighteen) the executor, unless a separate trustee has been appointed, must open a trustee account and act as trustee until the beneficiary reaches maturity. Advice should be sought from a Professional Financial Adviser.

Where no mortgage exists transfer of ownership has to be arranged. Again it is recommended that you use a solicitor but if you wish to arrange it personally the local Land Registry Office should be contacted.

There is no liability to Capital Gains Tax and the base price for beneficiaries (the figure which will be used to work out any future liability) is the value at the date of death.

RECORDS

It is essential that executors prepare (and sign) accounts showing exactly what has taken place and when. This written record acts as a safeguard to show that the executor acted properly and in good faith. It is especially important if there is likely to be trouble in the family.

All papers should be kept for a period of twelve years.

OUTLINE OF OBTAINING PROBATE

* Register Death
* Obtain Death Certificate
* Obtain details of all assets
* Value assets
* Discover details of all debts
* Prepare a detailed list of both
* Work out liability to IHT
* Arrange overdraft for IHT
* Prepare documents for probate registry
* Sign all documents
* Pay IHT
* Obtain Grant of Probate or
* Letters of Administration
* Send photocopies of grant to
* Bank insurance companies etc.
* Collect whatever is due to the estate
* Sell any assets
* Pay all debts
* Hand over any bequests
* Pay legacies

DISTRIBUTE OR INVEST THE RESIDUE

HELPFUL BOOKLETS

IR 45   Income Tax, Capital Gains Tax, Inheritance Tax guidance
FB 29   Help when someone dies (a guide to Social Security benefits)
Claim Form   (for Widows) BW 1
Claim Form   (for funeral expenses) SF 200
Claim Form   (for Widowed Mothers Allowance) NP 36
Claim Form   (for Widow's Pension) NP 36
Claim Form   (for Widow's Retirement Pension) NP 32A
Claim Form   (for Widow's Invalidity Benefit Employee) SSP 1 T or SSP 1 E
    Helpful Booklet NI 16 A
Claim Form   (for Widow's Invalidity Benefit Other than Employee) SSP 1 T or SSP 1 E – Helpful Booklet NI 16 A
Claim Form   (for War Widows) MPL 152 and MPL 154
Claim Form   (if husband died as a result of an accident at work) B 1
Claim Form   (if husband died as a result of certain diseases) PN 1

HELP FOR WIDOWERS OR OTHER RELATIVES

Retirement Pension   (IF LESS THAN FULL RATE PAID MAY QUALIFY FOR A TOP UP) Forms NP 32A and BD 8
Claim Form   (for Widower's Invalidity Benefit Other than Employee) SSP 1 T or SSP 1 E – Helpful Booklet NI 16 A
Claim Form   (for Widower's Invalidity Benefit Employee) SSP 1 T or SSP 1 E – Helpful Booklet NI 16 A
Claim Form   (if wife died as a result of an accident at work) B 1 200
Claim Form   (if wife died as a result of certain diseases) PN 1

HELP FOR ONE PARENT FAMILIES
Claim Form   CH 11

HELP FOR GUARDIANS
Claim Form   BG 1 and NI 14

SUPPLEMENTARY BENEFIT
Claim Form SB 1

FAMILY INCOME SUPPLEMENT
Claim Form FIS 1

HOUSING BENEFIT
Claim Form   RR 1

HELP WITH HEATING COSTS
Claim Form   SB 17 or SB 17A

TAX
Claim Form   IR 23

OTHER BENEFITS
Free Milk for Children under School Age   Form MV 11
Free Prescriptions   Form P 11 NHS Prescriptions
Free Dental Treatment   Form D 11 NHS Dental Treatment
Eyes   Form G 11 NHS Vouchers for glasses
Fares to Hospital if Child is ill   Form H 11 Fares to
   Hospital

If any difficulty in obtaining leaflets write to: Leaflets Unit, PO Box 21, Stanmore, Middlesex HA7 1AY

LIST OF PROBATE FORMS
Cap 44, Cap 40, Cap 37, PA 1, PA 2.

USEFUL ADDRESSES
Probate Personal Application Department (head office), 5th Floor, Golden Cross House, Ducannon Street, London WC2
Tel 071 210 4595

Public Trust Office, Stewart House, 24 Kingsway, London WC2B 6JX Tel 071 269 7000

COUNSELLING AND ADVISORY SERVICES
Age Concern (head office), Bernard Sunley House, 60 Pitcain Road, Mitcham, Surrey CR4 3LL
National Association of Widows, 54-57 Allison Street, Digbeth, Birmingham B5 5TH
Cruse (advice and counselling for widows and their children) Cruze House, 126 Sheen Road, Richmond, Surrey TW9 1UR

Capital Taxes Office, Minford House, Rockley Road, London W14 Tel 071 603 4622

Money Management Council, 18 Doughty Street, London WC1N 2PL

APPENDIX i

WIDOWS AND WIDOWERS

'The most loving act a man can do is to teach his wife how to be a widow'

This appendix is aimed mainly at widows for two reasons:

1. Women in general live longer than men, and it follows that there are many more widows than widowers. In fact, the average wife has nine years of widowhood in front of her, all too often with insufficient financial support.

2. Widows are literally left holding the baby with no paddle to help them. Even today, men still tend to be the main, and often the only breadwinner.

Therefore would it be a good idea to start a 'School for Widows'?

Although there is not, to my knowledge, a school for widows, there are several organizations who can and do help emotionally. However, since they only appear relevant after the event, they cannot help financially; it is often a case of too little, too late.

Prevention is better than cure: many of the financial problems could be averted, or at least made much more manageable, thus leaving the 'help' organizations to do what they are better equipped to do – help emotionally.

ON THE DEATH OF A LOVED ONE

The first feeling is often one of confusion, combined with an intense grief. A numbness sets in that prevents firm action, but carries the widow through the trauma of the funeral, although she may feel as though she herself is a witness at another person's time of grief.

The widow may feel that she has been deserted, and subsequently resent the departed loved ones but at the same time be unable to shake off a sense of guilt.

Some widows experience lethargy; some feel isolated, or are regarded as fair game by predatory men and feel uncomfortable socially without their usual companion. Other widows rush about in a frenzy, either doing nothing or polishing the table four times a day.

However, from the remains of a couple emerges a shattered self that has to be rebuilt and strengthened, and arise as a new integrated person.

A second and more stable stage now occurs as the widow starts to recover, but strangely when recovery is 'complete' a long term loneliness can set in. Widows often do not wish to impose on their children. Often treated as second class citizens, they are awkward and unwelcome at social events. They can even – and often do – have a feeling of guilt towards their dead husband if they enjoy themselves.

Financial problems can make all the above even worse. All too many widows suffer an alarming drop in their standard of living, just at a time when their emotions are at a low ebb. Things that were commonplace and taken for granted now become unaffordable luxuries as one salary or pension replaces two.

A little planning now can save a tremendous amount of anguish and deprivation in the future.

It is estimated that the average widow needs about 70 per cent of the previous income to maintain a comparable standard of living.

It is suggested that all couples set at least one 'contingency day' aside each year to review fully their family financial situation.

A check-list should be prepared.

1. Have you a budget? If so, is it adhered to? Is it working? How much extra should you allow for inflation?

2. Do you know what your financial position would be in the event of your spouse's death or long term injury?

3. What is your tax position?

4. Are all your debts protected (not just the mortgage)?

5. Is your Will up-to-date?

6. Do you have a copy of *'SPRATT'S GUIDE TO FINANCIAL RECORDING AND PLANNING'* or something similar?

7. Are your retirement plans on course?

8. Have you provided for your children's future?

9. Have you arranged for trustees/guardians/executors, where necessary?

and so many other items.

DO IT. YOU WILL FIND IT WELL WORTHWHILE

APPENDIX ii

IS YOUR MORTGAGE IN A STRAIT-JACKET?

The following is not intended to suggest that endowment is the best method of house purchase, but shows that, no matter how carefully the choice is made, even an apparently simple decision is full of potential pitfalls for the unwary.

There are basically two examples of Endowment:

With Profits

With the majority of this type of Endowment, neither the death benefit nor the term of the policy can be changed.

The increase options are generally in the form of an additional policy, which may carry its own extra policy charge and needs to be medically underwritten.

The growth is steady and secure, but if the policy is surrendered before it has run its full term, little or no terminal bonus is paid.

This means that this type of policy should always run its full term to receive the best value.

Thus, if you move home three times, provided that you have not cancelled any, you can end up with four policies (and often four policy fees) all tied to the same termination date.

Unit linked

With the majority of this type of policy, both the term and the death benefit can be modified to suit your changing requirements, in most cases without the need for further medical evidence. So, when you move home, adapt the premium and the term of the policy in line with your new needs. There is therefore only one policy charge.

A Unit linked policy gives you the choice of a wide range of investment areas, but as the surrender value is always the bid value of the units, you always receive the full value whenever you cancel the policy (however, this is not intended as a recommendation to cancel early as the longer you invest, the greater the chance of a high return). With many companies you receive a letter informing you when the fund is sufficient to repay your debt, (it is around the twenty year point on a twenty-five year term) giving you the opportunity to repay early and save interest. The growth of this type of investment is not as secure as that With profits, as the value can fall as well as rise, but having said that, many companies offer a 'With Profits' fund which has, in most cases, the advantages of both worlds.

Please look at the following pages with care and ensure that your next mortgage adviser gives the matter full consideration.

WEALTH WARNING: PLEASE DISCUSS THOROUGHLY WITH YOUR PROFESSIONAL ADVISER BEFORE ANY ACTION IS TAKEN.

ANOTHER WAY TO LOOK AT YOUR NEW MORTGAGE
(M £60,000)

The usual way to buy a new home is through an Endowment Mortgage on a Joint Life First Death basis. At first glance this would seem to make sense for if either party dies the outstanding mortgage is repaid. If both die, the mortgage is repaid but there is no cash surplus for the children. If both live to the end of the term, the mortgage is repaid together with a tax free lump sum but THE FULL VALUE OF THE HOME ALWAYS GOES INTO THE ESTATE FOR INHERITANCE TAX (IHT) PURPOSES ON THE SECOND TO DIE. WOULD IT BE BETTER IF: a more IHT efficient route was used?

EFFECT: on the first to die the remaining spouse has a choice:

1. Receives a tax free lump sum to repay the mortgage; OR

2. As the mortgage is a tax efficient loan and the repayments can be afforded the remaining spouse may wish to keep it and use the money in other ways. If the cash is not needed leave it in trust (tax free) for the children for school fees. This can be very useful in IHT planning.

3. The spouse still has life protection and the value of the investment.

With route 1 the house is always repaid without any option.

EFFECT: On the death of both together (or the second death):

4. The loan becomes a debt on the estate reducing the potential IHT by 40 per cent of the loan and transferring all the investment value and life protection tax free immediately to the beneficiaries, without any probate delays.

5. The financial effect, if both die on the first day of the mortgage, is that £136,750 is transferred immediately and tax free without any probate delay to the beneficiaries because the loan is now a debt on the estate it reduces the potential IHT payable by £24,000.

A TOTAL INCREASE IN TRANSFER OF £160,750

6. The financial effect, if both die one day before the end of the term, is that £211,000 is transferred immediately and tax free without any probate delays to the beneficiaries leaving the loan as a debt on the estate again reducing the potential IHT by £24,000

A TOTAL INCREASE IN TRANSFER OF £235,000

With route 1 the house would be paid for and be an asset to the estate the same would apply to any surplus value in the endowment.

COMPARATIVE COST

	J.L.F.D	ROUTE 2
Interest payment	£481.25 pm	£481.25 pm
Investment contribution	£ 95.24 pm	£100.47 pm
	£576.49 pm	£581.72 pm

7. If both survive:
A tax free surplus of £36,200   £36,100

ANOTHER WAY TO LOOK AT YOUR NEW MORTGAGE
(P £60,000)

The usual way to buy a new home is through an Endowment Mortgage on a Joint Life First Death basis. At first glance this would seem to make sense for if either party dies the outstanding mortgage is repaid. If both die the mortgage is paid. There is no cash surplus for the children. If both live then the loan is repaid together with a tax free lump sum BUT THE FULL VALUE OF THE HOME ALWAYS GOES INTO THE ESTATE ON THE SECOND TO DIE FOR INHERITANCE TAX PURPOSES. Also there is no tax efficient way of enjoying the fruits of your investment until the end of the term. WOULD IT BE BETTER IF: another route was used?

EFFECT: If either or both live, tax free lump sum will be paid:

In year 6	£ 3,000	In year 10	£ 6,000
In year 15	£16,000	In year 20	£32,000

In year twenty-five the home is repaid PLUS A TAX FREE LUMP SUM OF £67,000

EFFECT: On the first to die the remaining spouse has choice.

1. Receives a tax free lump sum immediately: to repay the mortgage OR
2. As the mortgage is a tax efficient loan and if the repayments can be afforded the remaining spouse may wish to keep it and use the money in other ways. If the cash is not needed leave it in trust (tax free) for the children for school fees or for Inheritance Tax planning.
3. The remaining spouse still has life protection and the value of the investment plan.

With route 1 home repaid only. No choice

EFFECT: On the death of both together (or the second death)

4. The loan becomes a debt on the estate, money from the life policies is transferred immediately and tax free to the beneficiaries.
5. The financial effect, if both die on the first day of the

mortgage is that £120,000 is transferred immediately tax free to the beneficiaries. The investment plan puts £23,400 into the estate which leaves a debt on the estate of £36,000 thus reducing the potential IHT by £14,640.

A TOTAL INCREASE IN TRANSFER OF £134,640

6. The financial effect, if both die one day before the end of term is that the investment plan repays the Mortgage plus £67,000. £120,000 is transferred immediately and tax free to the beneficiaries.

A TOTAL INCREASE IN TRANSFER OF £120,000

With route 1 home repaid plus any values of the Endowment into the estate.

COMPARATIVE COST

	J.L.F.D.	J.L.S.D.
Interest payment	£481.25 pm	£481.25 pm
Contribution	£ 95.24 pm	£125.47 pm*
If both survive:	£576.49 pm	£606.72 pm
7. A Tax Free surplus of	£36,200	£67,000

(*£100 of this increases at 10 per cent pa for fifteen years)

ANOTHER WAY TO LOOK AT YOUR NEW MORTGAGE (SL)

The usual way to buy a new home is through an Endowment Mortgage on a Joint Life First Death basis. At first glance this would seem to make sense for if either party dies the outstanding mortgage is repaid but, the remaining partner has no protection for the children. If both die the mortgage is repaid leaving no cash surplus for the children. On the second to die the value of the house is always in the estate leaving a potential Inheritance Tax (IHT) liability (£24,000 in this example - 40 per cent of £60,000). No thought ever is given to the IHT implications.

WOULD IT BE BETTER IF: another route was chosen?
EFFECT: CHOICE
If the breadwinner dies first:
1. The spouse has the mortgage repaid but still has protection on his or her life.
If the spouse dies the breadwinner has the tax free cash:
2. To repay the mortgage OR
3. As the mortgage is a tax efficient loan and if the repayments can be afforded they may wish to keep it and use the money in other ways eg. if the cash is not needed leave it (£60,000 in this example) in trust (tax free) for the beneficiaries to use for, say, school fees – also could be very useful in IHT planning as the money would not form part of the estate for IHT purposes nor would there be any Probate delay.
4. The remaining breadwinner also still has the value of an investment plan and protection on their life.
EFFECT: if both die together on the day the mortgage taken out:
5. The home is repaid and a lump sum is immediately transferred tax free to the beneficiaries without any probate delays (£60,000 in this example).
EFFECT: if both die one day before the mortgage is due to be repaid.
6. The home is repaid plus £36,200 paid into the estate plus an immediate tax free payment to the beneficiaries of £60,000.

A TOTAL INCREASE IN TRANSFER TO THE BENEFICIARIES OF £60,000

COMPARATIVE COSTS

	J.L.F.D.	ROUTE 2
Interest payment	£481.25 pm	£481.25 pm
Additional contribution	£ 95.24 pm	£ 97.49 pm
	£576.49 pm	£578.74 pm

EFFECT: if both live until the end of the term:
7. Tax free surplus   £36,200*   £36,200*

(* Assumes 10.5 per cent growth)

APPENDIX iii

COMPARISON OF: TAXED AND NON-TAXED GROWTH

(25 PER CENT TAXPAYER)

Net amount to be invested is £1000:

	Taxed	Non-Taxed	Pension
Gross Investment	£ 1,000	£ 1,000	£ 1,333
Tax returned	Nil	Nil	£ 333
Net Investment	£ 1,000	£ 1,000	£ 1,000
Gross Interest	13.3%	13.3%	13.3%
Net Interest	10.0%	13.3%	13.3%

Return After (to the nearest £10):

5 Years	£ 1,600	£ 1,860	£ 2,480
10 Years	£ 2,590	£ 3,490	£ 4,640
15 Years	£ 4,180	£ 6,510	£ 8,660
20 Years	£ 6,730	£ 2,150	£16,160
25 Years	£10,830	£22,690	£30,170

It takes almost FOUR years for a Building Society (taxed) type investment to reach the point at which a Pension investment STARTS. As can be seen from the above there is no other investment that is as tax efficient as a pension scheme.

COMPARISON OF: TAXED AND NON-TAXED GROWTH

(40 PER CENT TAXPAYER)

Net amount to be invested is £1000:

	Taxed	Non-Taxed	Pension
Gross Investment	£ 1,000	£ 1,000	£ 1,667
Tax returned	Nil	Nil	£ 667
Net Investment	£ 1,000	£ 1,000	£ 1,000
Gross Interest	13.3 %	13.3%	13.3%
Net Interest	7.98%	13.3%	13.3%

Return After (to the nearest £10):

5 Years	£ 1,470	£ 1,860	£ 3,110
10 Years	£ 2,160	£ 3,490	£ 5,810
15 Years	£ 3,160	£ 6,510	£10,850
20 Years	£ 4,640	£12,150	£20,260
25 Years	£ 6,820	£22,690	£37,820

It takes over FIVE years for a Building Society (taxed) type investment to reach where a Pension investment STARTS. As can be seen from the above there is no other investment that is as tax efficient as a pension scheme.

    Tax Relief on the investment
    Tax Free Growth
    Tax Free Cash
    Pension Guaranteed for Life
    Inland Revenue Protected

To gain these advantages the only penalty is that the pension cannot be taken before age fifty. The actual return of £1000 invested (as at January 1989 figures by BZW)

	10 years	15 years	20 years
EQUITIES	£3,120 (12.1%)	£3,290 (8.3%)	£3,710 (5.4%)
BUILDING SOCIETY	£ 950 (−0.5%)	£ 640 (−2.9%)	£ 550 (−2.3%)
GILTS	£1,760 (5.8%)	£1,580 (3.1%)	£1,080 (0.3%)

APPENDIX iv

HOW MUCH WILL I EARN DURING MY WORKING LIFETIME?

During our lifetime most of us will earn a fortune.

How much will you have left for your retirement?

Years to Retirement	\multicolumn{6}{c}{Present Annual Salary £ assuming an increase of 7.5% pa}
	6,000	8,000	10,000	12,000	14,000	16,000
5	34,000	46,467	58,084	69,701	81,317	92,934
10	84,883	113,177	141,471	169,765	198,059	226,353
15	156,710	208,947	261,184	313,420	365,657	417,894
20	259,828	346,437	433,047	519,656	606,266	692,875
25	407,867	543,823	679,734	815,734	951,690	1,087,646
30	620,396	827,195	1,033,994	1,240,793	1,447,592	1,654,390
40	925,510	1,234,013	1,542.516	1,851,019	2,159,522	2,468,026
45	1,992,387	2,656,516	3,320,645	3,984,774	4,648,903	5,313,032

Most of this will be spent

How much will you keep for yourself?

How much will your family get if you died today?

How much would you want them to have?

HOW MUCH WILL YOU NEED TO LAST FOURTEEN YEARS OF RETIREMENT?*

---

* average life expectancy of a male retiring at age sixty-five

APPENDIX v

THE COST OF DELAYING SAVINGS AND LIFE PROTECTION

The cost of waiting can be catastrophic. For example, a man aged thirty-two would like to save £1000 on an annual basis. He also wishes to protect his family from the economic crisis that would occur if he were to die unexpectedly. To accomplish that he would need to provide an income of £15,000 pa (a capital sum of £150,000).

The illustration above is based on a 10 per cent growth, and shows that if he waited one year before he started saving and investing (ie. to age thirty-three) the loss at age sixty-five would be £29,134. If he waited just one month the loss would be £2428; if one week, the loss would be £560; if one day, the loss would be £80. Now we are only talking of investing £2.74 per day.

If he were to die during the waiting period the loss to his family would be £150,000.

THE COST OF DELAY ON THE INVESTMENT RETURN

1 year	£29,134
1 month	£ 2,428
1 week	£ 560
1 day	£ 80

IF DEATH OCCURRED AT ANY TIME DURING THE WAITING PERIOD THE LOSS WOULD BE:

1 year	£150,000
1 month	£150,000
1 week	£150,000
1 day	£150,000

DOES IT MAKE SENSE TO WAIT?

APPENDIX vi

AIMS OF THE BOOK

1. To show people the importance of Financial Planning

2. To encourage people to take an active interest in their Financial Planning

3. To remove the mystery surrounding Financial Planning

4. To help in the selection of a Financial Adviser

5. To show people the problems and expense that result from:
   a. of not planning
   b. of ad hoc planning
   c. of choosing a poor adviser

6. To show the importance of Wills in all Financial Planning

7. To help their executors, trustees and guardians in the event of a death

8. To assist other professionals in the course of their work

9. How to reduce the financial impact in the event of your death

10. To bring the whole family to help

11. To help people decide what they want from life, financially

12. To help them achieve what they want from life, financially

13. To give them peace of mind knowing that their loved ones will be looked after in the manner they would like whether they are here or not

14. To help Widows and Widowers at a time of great stress

APPENDIX vii

GENERAL COMMENTS

I was visiting a friend and their young child was being a nuisance so I tore up a map of the world into small pieces and said, 'Please put it back together.' To my surprise she was back again in a few minutes with the map fully and correctly put together again. When I asked her how she had done it she just turned the map over to show a picture of herself and said:
   'I just put myself back together and the world was put right.'
   This, of course, is not true, but it does make you think.

WHAT IS SUCCESS?
Most people misunderstand success.
   A successful person is one who has failed more often than someone who is not successful. Most people fail to understand that success is a journey and not a destination, that as soon as you start to plan you start to be successful.

WHAT IS FAILURE?
Most people misunderstand failure.
   The only true failure is by those who do not try. To try and not succeed is not failure; the only true failure is not to try for there is always tomorrow. All that has happened is that you have lost a battle not the war.
   Have you ever watched a tennis match when one player has been two sets down and three games to love and they have still won the match?

IF THIS BOOK HAS NOT:
* made you think
* made you plan
* made you act

THEN IT HAS FAILED – FOR YOU.

In this case please pass it on to someone else who may benefit from it.

Please write to me and let me know why it has not helped you

IF THIS BOOK HAS:
* made you think
* made you plan
* made you act

it has succeeded in its aim.

Please write to me and let me know how it has helped.

APPENDIX viii

THE STORY BEHIND THE FIGURES

1. 91 per cent of policies are incorrect in some detail

This is an indictment of the quality of financial advice given at all levels.

2. 87 per cent do not have the age of the policyholder proved

This may appear to be very unimportant but let us look at the effect in the case of a joint life first death endowment in the event of the husband's premature death.

Stage 1	Obtain death certificate	1 week
Stage 2	Send death certificate to insurance company	2 weeks
Stage 3	Company writes to say client dead, but when was client born?	3 weeks
Stage 4	Widow sends his birth certificate	4 weeks
Stage 5	Company writes and asks for marriage certificate	5 weeks
Stage 6	Widow sends marriage certificate	6 weeks
Stage 7	Company asks for her birth certificate	7 weeks
Stage 8	Widow sends her birth certificate*	8 weeks
Stage 9	Company send a cheque	9 weeks

---

* If the widow has been married before then the company will ask her to prove her identity which can sometimes be quite a problem because on divorce her marriage certificate is taken away and not all divorce certificates put the maiden name on. This costs yet more time.

By now two or three months interest has accrued and so there is insufficient to clear the loan without taking capital from elsewhere (that is if she has it).

True this does not always happen, but think of all the emotional, as well as financial problems this so often overlooked point causes when it does happen.

Now I do agree that the insurance company does need proof of birth and marriage but it should be done at the beginning not at the end so would it not be much better to prove ages at the outset of the policy? Yet in 87 per cent of policies this problem can occur.

The trouble is that advisers and insurance companies are too keen to get the business on the books and either do not realize the potential problems or do not care. I am not sure which is the worst of these two possible scenarios.

3 & 4. Use of Trusts with Pensions and Life Assurance.
The effect of using a trust is twofold:
1. in the case of a husband dying with a Will then the monies go direct to the widow without any probate delay (ie. immediately instead of after three to six months).
2. in the case of a husband dying without a Will it ensures that the widow receives all the money immediately (if no Will and no trust then the rules of intestacy prevail and the widow is only entitled to £75,000 if there are children and then after about six months wait).
3. if both parents die then the children receive the money immediately and tax free. If no trust used then the children would have to wait for probate and then pay 40 per cent tax on any monies over £140,000.

5. Savings plans
Now a very small point but it used to be very important before legislation changed.

6. 68 per cent of executive pensions are not set up correctly
Because of an error in the way around 68 per cent of executive pension schemes have been formed there are three problems–
1. the scheme is not legal

2. in the event if the executive dying the company may retain, for its own purposes, the death in service benefit instead of giving it to the widow

3. in the event of the member retiring the company can again retain the monies for its own benefit and not pay them to the retired member.

Even if you do not mind that your widow may not benefit I am confident that you would appreciate your pension being paid.

These three possible situations are not very pleasant and yet 68 per cent of schemes fall into one of the three categories.

7. 81 per cent of partnerships have no protection
Without this the chances are that you will be in partnership with your dead partner's widow or someone of her choice.

8. 69 per cent of limited companies have no share protection
Without this your widow could (whilst owning your shares) have no income at all from them and when she dies your children will have to pay Inheritance Tax on your shareholding yet possibly derive no income from that shareholding.

9. 79 per cent of companies have no protection for their key people
Yet most businesses would suffer a severe setback on the loss of, say, a top salesperson or production manager. Bank loans may be called in.

10. 76 per cent of people do not have a Will
Yet without a Will your assets will not go where you want them to, more tax will be paid than needs to and delays will be caused. It is probable that your widow will not be your largest beneficiary.

11. IHT planning and mortgages
If mortgages – even small ones – are not planned correctly then your children could pay more Inheritance Tax than they need to.

Yet I have not found another adviser that plans a mortgage with any thought of the IHT effects. This oversight can mean that as much as 40 per cent of the mortgage can be lost to the estate in IHT.